Tanzania Political Economy series, 2

OVERCOMING CONSTRAINTS ON TANZANIAN GROWTH

Policy Challenges Facing the Third Phase Government

Edited by
Professor Samuel M. Wangwe
and
Professor Brian Van Arkadie

MKUKI NA NYOTA PUBLISHERS
DAR ES SALAAM

Published for the Economic and Social Research Foundation by
Mkuki na Nyota Publishers
6 Muhonda Street, Mission Quarter, Kariakoo
P.O. Box 4246, Dar es Salaam
Tanzania

© Economic and Social Research Foundation (2000)

ISBN 9976 973 78 0

Distributed outside Africa by
African Books Collective Ltd
27 Park End Street
Oxford OX1 1HU
UK

Table of contents

This book benefited from the contribution of many people. The consultants who prepared first drafts of various chapters include Mr. Deo Mutalemwa, Dr. Joseph Shitundu, Dr. Eliab Luvanda and Dr. Godwin Mjema. The research staff of ESRF, in particular Dr. Haji Semboja, Dr. Flora Musonda, Dr. Paula Tibandebage and Dr. Yvonne Tsikata, made comments on various drafts of this work. Members of the ESRF Policy Forum made useful suggestions at a dinner presentation by Prof. Wangwe in October 1999, as did DFID staff in December 1999 in Dar es Salaam. Professors Brian Van Arkadie and Samuel Wangwe put together the final report.

Miss Lorah Madete and Miss Hellen Lawuo provided research assistance, wrote first drafts of some sections of the report and managed the logistics involved in coordinating inputs into the study.

The ESRF would like to thank DFID for the grant that made it possible to meet costs of this work.

List of tables

ADB	African Development Bank
AIDS	Acquired Immune Deficiency Syndrome
ALAF	Aluminium Africa Limited
ALP	Agricultural and Livestock Policy
AMAP	Aid Management and Accountability Programme
ATC	Air Tanzania Corporation
BFIA	Banking and Financial Institutions Act
BOP	Balance of Payments
BOT	Bank of Tanzania
CCM	Chama Cha Mapinduzi
CIS	Commodity Import Support
CMSA	Capital Market and Securities Authority
COMSEC	Commonwealth Secretariat
CRDB	Co-operative and Rural Development Bank
DFID	Department for International Development
DSE	Dar es Salaam Stock Exchange
EC	European Commission
ERP	Economic Recovery Programme
ESAF	Enhanced Structural Adjustment Facility
ESRF	Economic and Social Research Foundation
EU	European Union
GDP	Gross Domestic Product
GOT	Government of Tanzania
HIPC	Highly Indebted Poor Countries
HIV	Human Immuno-deficiency Virus
IFI	International Financial Institutions
ILO-IPRE	International Labour Organisation -Investment for Poverty Reducing Employment
IMF	International Monetary Fund
IMTC	Inter Ministerial Technical Committee
IPC	Investment Promotion Centre
IPO	Initial Public Offering
IRP	Integrated Road Programme
IT	Information Technology
ITC	International Trade Conference
LART	Loans and Advances Realisation Trust
MDF	Multilateral Debt Relief Fund
MOH	Ministry of Health
MP	Member of Parliament
MTEF	Mid-Term Expenditure Framework
NAEP II	National Agricultural Extension Programme
NALRP	National Agriculture and Livestock Research Project

NBC	National Bank of Commerce
NCPI	National Consumer Price Index
NDC	National Development Corporation
NEP	National Employment Policy
NGO	Non Governmental Organisation
NIPPA	National Investment Promotion and Protection Act
NLP	New Land Policy
NMB	National Microfinance Bank
ODA	Overseas Development Assistance
OECD	Organisation of Economic Co-operation and Development
OGL	Open General License
PBZ	People's Bank of Zanzibar
PCB	Prevention of Corruption Bureau
PER	Public Expenditure Review
PFP	Policy Framework Paper
PHAST	Participatory Hygiene and Sanitation Transformation
PIU	Project Implementation Unit
PMU	Project Management Unit
PSRC	Parastatal Sector Reform Commission
PSRP	Public Service Reform Programme
PT	Privatisation Trust
RPFB	Rolling Plan and Forward Budget
SADC	Southern Africa Development Community
SHERSP	Southern Highlands Extension and Rural Financial Services
SIDO	Small Industries Development Organisation
SSA	Sub-Saharan Africa
SSR	Social Sector Review
SSS	Social Sector Strategy
TA	Technical Assistance
TANESCO	Tanzania Electric Supply Company
TARP II	Tanzania Agriculture Research Project
TAS	Tanzania Assistance Strategy
TCC	Tanzania Cigarette Company
THB	Tanzania Housing Bank
TIB	Tanzania Investment Bank
TIC	Tanzania Investment Centre
TPB	Tanzania Postal Bank
TRA	Tanzania Revenue Authority
TTCL	Tanzania Telecommunication Company Limited
UK	United Kingdom
UN	United Nations
UNCTAD	United Nations Conference for Trade and Development

UNDP	United Nations Development Programme
UNHCR	United Nations High Commissioner for Refugees
USA	United States of America
VETA	Vocational Education Training Authority
WFP	World Food Programme
WB	World Bank
WHO	World Health Organisation
WTO	World Trade Organisation

Background

This work is an attempt to place the economic performance of Mkapa's Third Phase Government within the context of current constraints and the social, economic and political situation it inherited on taking office. The study is based on an interpretative review of existing literature and research on the Tanzanian economy. Several papers were commissioned, interviews made with key players in the Tanzanian economy and a synthesis was produced based on these contributions.

The report is being completed at a particularly interesting point in Tanzanian history. The death of Mwalimu Nyerere, the founding father and dominant political figure of the past four decades, ends an era just as a new century begins and the Third Phase Government enters the final year of its first term. It is an appropriate moment to look backwards and forwards, and this study attempts to do both.

The policies of the past four years have continued a process of change and adjustment began in the mid-1980s, in the face of economic crisis created over the first generation of Tanzanian independence. The policy options facing the government have to be understood in relation to the nature of that system and the crisis it faced, and the underlying constraints on the country's economic growth. However, this short study does not purport to write the history of the evolution, successes and failures of Tanzanian economic policies since independence. A balanced assessment of the Nyerere era, for example, has still to be written. Interestingly, the goals espoused in the Arusha Declaration of equality, self-help and inclusive development continue to have strong resonance in current discussions of poverty and development policies. It is still too early to judge whether these goals will be more readily achievable in the context of a liberalised economy. There is a need to sort out the record of the seventies, to assess what the key failures were, which, alongside a hostile external environment, caused the crisis of the regime.

The disruption of agricultural markets, over-reliance on bureaucratic parastatals and failure to adjust macroeconomic policies in a timely fashion, all contributed to the economic crisis of the 1970s and 1980s. How far these mistakes were inherent in the Arusha Declaration, and how far they could have been avoided, while still retaining the core aspirations espoused in 1967, remains a fitting subject for future debate.

Whatever the interpretation of its origins, the extended impact of the crisis and the resulting economic cul-de-sac in which the country found itself in the early 1980s still influences the current policy agenda. The government has struggled to put in place fiscal, monetary and foreign exchange policies to achieve a reasonable degree of internal and external macroeconomic balance. The reform of the post-Arusha economic institutions remains incomplete. The government machine, weakened by over-ambition and by the strains of economic crisis and adjustment, faces the challenge of rebuilding its capacity. While slow improvements in incentives may render the civil service slogan "the government pretends to pay us, and we pretend to work" redundant, after years of restrictions on recruitment the public service is ageing and morale is low. The popular aspirations for access to basic services and a better life, to which the Arusha Declaration responded, have still to be realised.

This short study has a selective focus, but it is hoped that the themes covered will deepen understanding of economic policy issues in Tanzania. The book is organised as follows:

> **Chapter 1** addresses the prospects of raising the rate of economic growth, examining key challenges in agriculture, exports, capital formation and human and institutional development.
>
> **Chapter 2** examines the status of the social delivery system (education, health and water). Some of the most profound changes in institutions in recent years have related to social service provision. Supply through state monopoly had sought (but failed) to achieve universal provision of basic services. That approach is now being displaced by a mixed system of public and private provision, the welfare implications of which are not yet evident.
>
> **Chapter 3** examines developments in monetary policy and the financial sector.
>
> **Chapter 4** looks at the potential contribution of the private sector to Tanzanian growth.
>
> **Chapter 5** addresses issues of governance and public sector development.
>
> **Chapter 6** discusses donor relations. Over the past three decades, during which trade and private investment linkages with the global economy weakened, aid dependency increased. The negative influence of aid on national capabilities and the distortion of incentives resulting from aid dependence are a source of deep concern.

Combating Poverty: the ultimate goal

The paramount objective of growth is the reduction of poverty. Tanzania has been classified as one of the poorest countries in the World, with a per capita income of US $180. Other economic objectives, such as GDP growth, price stability, stable exchange rates and fiscal balance, should be seen as the means to achieve poverty reduction.

It is estimated that as many as half of Tanzanians live in poverty. The majority of Tanzania's population, and most of the country's poor live in rural areas. It has been estimated that as many as 90 percent of the poorest people live in rural areas. Incomes in rural areas depend largely on the prosperity of the household farms. Regions that have successful producers of perennial crops have tended to be better off; coffee and tea producing areas are generally quite prosperous rural communities. Whereas the most intractable poverty is in areas where inhospitable soils and uncertain rainfall restrict potential farm productivity and incomes. However, these are not the only decisive factors: AIDS has had a deeply negative impact on many rural areas, including previously prosperous communities.

In a country with a low level of output, such as Tanzania, widespread poverty is the inevitable result of low productivity, and is therefore to be explained as a result of the country's low level of development. This is not to say that economic growth inevitably leads to the eradication of poverty - some countries have experienced growth without a commensurate reduction in poverty, and even in very rich countries pockets of poverty persist. However, although growth alone is not sufficient to reduce poverty, for a country at Tanzania's average income level economic growth is a necessary condition for poverty eradication.

It may be possible to direct aid and the government budget to meet the needs of the poor, but in a country at Tanzania's income level, it is difficult to sustain poverty programmes in the absence of growth. Even the progress Tanzania made in the 1970s, in relation to education and health, was not sustainable in the face of economic stagnation. In relation to most of the social indicators Tanzania has lost the gains it achieved in the 1970s, for example, in areas such as school enrolment. Income redistribution possibilities are strictly limited given the low average income and will have to concentrate on groups unable to help themselves (such as AIDS orphans).

If widespread poverty is the inevitable outcome of low national output, in what sense is it necessary to examine poverty eradication policies as a concern distinct from the study of constraints on growth more generally? The main reason a specific focus on poverty is required is that the poor often fall outside of the organised economy of successful cash crop agriculture and formal employment. A poverty strategy that relies on the growth of the formal sectors to generate income opportunities for the poor could leave most of them untouched. Therefore, the focus of a poverty strategy must be to find means whereby the poor can raise their productivity and income levels in their existing institutional setting. Such a strategy would seek to raise the rate of national output growth by providing greater opportunities to utilise a relatively abundant resource, labour, in wealth producing activities, thereby increasing the incomes of the poor through increasing their contribution to economic growth.

The liberalising policies under the Economic Recovery Programme (ERP) have had little effect on the incomes of the very poor. The immediate negative impact of stabilisation measures has been on the formally employed, who were not among the poorest sector of society. In some ways, the poorest of the poor lie too far outside the workings of the formal economy to be affected by macroeconomic policies concerned with sectoral terms of trade, incomes from formal employment and farm prices. However, the move away from the universal provision of social services and the introduction of user charges will have had an impact on the poor - as coverage of the education system declines, it is the poorest in society who are excluded.

The first target of a national effort to tackle poverty must be poor rural households. No breakthrough in poverty alleviation is likely to take place without raising agricultural output and reducing its instability. Poor rural households are highly vulnerable to the uncertainty of rain-fed agriculture. And lack of cash income leaves little possibility of defending family food security through market purchases. Therefore, a breakthrough in agricultural productivity is required, so that in good years agriculturists can produce a growing marketable surplus, and by so doing cushion themselves against the effects of setbacks in bad years.

The requirements for accelerated agricultural growth are discussed in Chapter 1. There is no potential 'Green Revolution' on hand that can transform productivity in the poorer farming communities at a stroke. Many earlier efforts to find short cuts to dramatically increase agricultural productivity have failed. This was the case in the 1940s, with the groundnut scheme; in the 1960s, with the Village Settlement Programme; in the 1970s, with the Ujamaa campaign and other various ambitious donor-backed efforts to increase agricultural productivity (the National Maize Programme) and improve rural conditions (rural water programmes). The improvements that were achieved resulted from mainly piece-meal improvements in farm productivity, not greatly affected by public policy and not well researched or understood.

The prime importance of poverty reduction has been recognised in Vision 2025, which advocates the eradication of poverty by the year 2025. The same concern was reflected in the National Poverty Eradication Strategy (June 1996), and has been endorsed by the policies of most donors. Poverty concerns have been expressed as an important guide in the formulation of the Poverty Reduction Policy Paper (replacing the Policy Framework Paper) and the Tanzania Assistance Strategy. For these concerns to be realised programmes will be required which respond to the needs and the potential of particular groups and areas, as opposed to ambitious national campaigns which have failed in the past.

In the face of limited resources, it will be wise for initial attention to be given to problems which are well understood and within the capability of the government and donors to solve. One key focus for government and donor policy should be to aid isolated rural communities by investing in their access to the rest of the economy. This should be done through investment in transport facilities, thereby reducing the cost of transport, enabling trade and increasing the strategies available to poor rural households.

For the poor who are unable to improve their lot on the shamba, the alternative is to seek employment. Formal employment in the economy is rather small, accounting for only about 8.6 percent of the total employment (Wangwe et al, 1998). The public sector is the main source of formal employment, with about 70 percent of formal employment in the 1990s. Though reliable data on employment growth in recent years is not available, the fact that its growth is not keeping up with the growth of the labour force is not disputed. Growth in formal employment has been weak. With between 400,000 and 600,000 job seekers every year, it is clear that employment opportunities are not coping with current demand.

Employment in the civil service and its parastatal sector has declined since 1993 as a direct result of civil service and parastatal reform. Between 1993 and 1996, over 61,000 government employees were retrenched. During the same period payment to 14,600 'ghost workers' was stopped. There was a hiring freeze for four years, which was partially lifted in July 1999. College and university students are no longer guaranteed jobs in the public sector on graduating. In the parastatal sector, the workforce declined from 308,000 in 1982 to 180,800 in 1993 and 176,000 in 1994. More recent figures are not available, but the number has continued to fall as a result of the on-going divestiture programme. Some of those who lost public sector jobs are likely to have joined the ranks of the poor.

Given that overall public sector employment is not expected to grow substantially in the near future, the country will have to rely increasingly on the private sector to provide jobs. Yet the prospects for the private sector absorbing large numbers of workers are not great in the immediate future. Only about 57,000 formal jobs were created in the private sector in 1998. In public enterprises being privatised, new management has to grapple with inherited over-staffing. Their first priorities must be to reduce the work force and increase labour productivity. Even if the existing formal private sector employment grows at 10 percent per annum (Vision 2025), only about 45,000 jobs would be generated per annum.

Annual employment growth (including self-employment in agriculture) over the next few years could be as follows: agriculture (at 3 percent employment growth) 230,000 jobs, the existing formal private sector 45,000 high growth sectors (mining and tourism) 60,000 and resumption of employment growth in the civil service (especially at local government level) at 10,000. The total comes to about 345,000 new jobs per year, based on an optimistic scenario. A more conservative estimate would give a figure of around quarter of a million. The labour market will be receiving between 400,000 and 600,000 new entrants each year.

In the absence of formal jobs, workers are assimilated into the informal sector. A survey of the informal sector in 1991 was supplemented by a further survey for Dar es Salaam in 1995. In 1991 about 2.4 million people were involved in the informal sector at some point during the year. Unemployment and the influx of unemployed youths into urban areas has had immense economic and social consequences. In previous governments, attempts were made to tackle this problem by direct action to repatriate migrants back to rural areas, and through mass mobilisation campaigns (*Uhuru na Kazi, Kazi ni Uhai, Kilimo cha Kufa na Kupona*). Such campaigns were not sustainable and rural-urban migration has not abated, with urban population increasing at about 6 percent per annum, a growth rate about twice the rate of population growth.

A comprehensive policy was outlined under the 1983 Human Resources Deployment Act. It recognised the fact that the formal sector was not going to solve the problem of unemployment alone. Self-employment and the informal sector had to be enhanced. Due to weak implementation and the violation of human rights, the results were poor. Based on a 1991 ILO recommendation the government, in 1997, presented a National Employment Policy (NEP) aiming to achieve the following:

(a) self-reliance among workers;
(b) promotion of employment;
(c) leadership on policy coordination and clarity of the roles of different actors (ministerial agencies, local government and the private sector); and
(d) provision of accurate information on the status of the labour market.

NEP has outlined strategies for five sectors and five special groups to achieve these objectives. The sectors include those where most employment is expected to be created, such as industry and trade, agriculture, commerce and services, and small-scale mining. The special groups are those who have been disadvantaged in employment practices such as women, youths, the disabled, and retrenched persons.

The National Employment Council (NEC) that was charged with the strategy's implementation had not taken off three years after the Cabinet approved the policy in April 1997. Moreover, the NEC is rather unwieldy, with eighteen member institutions and the intention to invite others from parastatal agencies and NGOs, such as VETA and SIDO, from universities, as well as the ILO and UNDP, to join. This and other inadequacies, including insufficient consultation and involvement of all parties engaged in employment has led to the decision to revisit and revise the NEP. At the time of publication, the revised NEP was being finalised.

Seeking to deal with the poverty issue in a sustained fashion, the government adopted the National Poverty Eradication Strategy policy in 1998. A new department was created in 1998 under the Vice President's office, with two related units - one for handling environmental matters and the other for dealing with poverty eradication. A minister of state now heads this department. Thus there are great efforts to devise policies and an aid strategy with a strong poverty eradication focus. The success of these efforts will depend on how far efforts by government and donors can identify significant new opportunities for poor rural dwellers and those in the urban informal sector to raise their productivity.

This report offers a cautionary note regarding what can be achieved. What emerges from a review of past experience is that the expenditure of government and donor energy on the production of reports, strategies and policies has too often failed to generate effective achievements on the ground. In recent years, policy has been effective to a degree in reducing government interference in the economy, and has been much less effective in designing and implementing new interventions. When confronted with an issue as worthy and challenging as national poverty eradication, the danger lies in the formulation of ambitious agendas with long lists of desirable but unrealistic activities. The lack of realism takes four forms:

(a) First, given the limited implementation capacity of government, clear priorities are required which focus on limited but achievable activities. This is rarely done.

(b) Second, programmes need to be founded on realistic assessments of the options on the ground, adjusted to local realities. The knowledge base is often inadequate for this, and is too readily replaced by global assumptions about viable strategies.

(c) Third, a careful analysis of the sustainability of project activities is needed. This is particularly necessary for interventions at the local level, where a realistic assessment is required of the capacity to operate and maintain project facilities.

(d) Finally, the agencies involved in development programmes need to be aware of their comparative advantage, and, limitations. It is particularly difficult for large donors to come to terms with the limits of their own capabilities. The record of donor involvement in Tanzania is replete

**with donor initiatives based on a gross misjudgement of their own
capacity.**

1. Basic constraints on economic growth

Economic growth as a necessary condition for development

The main objective of the economic reforms introduced in the mid-1980s and continued during the Third Phase Government has been to restore growth momentum to the economy. This was not because growth per se is the ultimate objective of policy. It became evident during the years of crisis that a growing economy is a necessary condition for the achievement of the ultimate objective of economic policy - the improvement of the living conditions of the mass of the population. The sustained expansion of education and health, broad based improvement in nutrition and increases in consumption all depend on an increase in per capita output.

Earlier literature has argued that it is possible to have growth without development - growth of the kind that enriches the few without providing improvement in the satisfaction of the basic needs of the mass of the population. Growth in the incomes of the wealthy does not necessarily 'trickle-down' to benefit the poor. There is a good deal of evidence in support of this argument, and it is important to recognise that growth in aggregate GDP is not a social end in itself. However, Tanzanian experience has also demonstrated how difficult it is to sustain development progress without growth in output. Assessment of the reforms that have been implemented during the Second and Third Phase Governments ultimately must be on success or failure in accelerating growth.

Performance and potential

The Third Phase Government came to power in November 1995, after ten years of policy reform implementation. The ERP for 1986/87 and 1988/89 mainly focused on economic liberalisation and stabilisation.The ERP included price and market reforms, liberalisation of the exchange rate and foreign trade regimes, and fiscal and industrial policy changes. With these reforms and with access to additional external support, the decline of the economy was halted and output growth initiated in most of the sectors of the economy. The Economic and Social Action Programme (ESAP), (1989/90-1991/92) sought to address social as well as economic issues.

From 1993/94 an attempt was made to increase the effectiveness of medium term economic management through a Rolling Plan and Forward Budget system (RPFB). Maintenance of macroeconomic stability was a top priority. The Third Phase Government came to power during the third year of the implementation of RPFB. The objectives of RPFB for the period up to 1998/99 included:

(a) real GDP growth of 5 percent in 1996/97, rising to 6 percent in 1997/98-1998/99;

(b)   reduction of inflation to 15 percent in 1996/97, 7.5 percent in 1997/98 and 5 percent in 1998/99; and

(c)   achieving a further decline in the external current account deficit.

GDP growth since 1987 is summarised in Table 1.

Table 1: Gross Domestic Product at 1992 Prices

Year	GDP (Tshs Million)	Per Capita GDP	Per Capita GDP Growth	Real GDP Growth (Annual change %)
1987	1,071,541	49,125	4.0	-
1988	1,119,017	49,553	0.9	4.4
1989	1,147,745	49,421	-0.3	2.6
1990	1,219,237	51,050	3.3	6.2
1991	1,253,132	51,021	-0.1	2.8
1992	1,275,916	50,514	-1.0	1.8
1993	1,281,007	49,315	-2.4	0.4
1994	1,298,942	48,625	-1.4	1.4
1995	1,345,247	48,987	0.7	3.6
1996	1,401,711	49,652	1.4	4.2
1997	1,448,089	49,898	0.5	3.3
1998	1,505,827	50,194	0.9	4.0

Source: BoT 1999

These figures suggest that after a spurt in growth during the ERP period, the momentum of the economy slowed. Per capita incomes fell between 1990 and 1994, and although that was followed by a modest revival, per capita income in 1998 was still below that of 1990. Annual growth rates fell short of the RPFB targets. While macroeconomic data is often unreliable, due to the questionable quality of some of the indices from which GDP is calculated, this evidence indicates that the growth achieved has been quite modest.

There are a number of possible explanations for this mediocre performance. Liberalisation in the mid-1980s generated a positive initial market response and the severe conditions of the early 1980s were eased. However, although markets were liberalised, the private sector remained dependent on public infrastructure. Disruptions in transport (associated with bad weather), and unreliable power and water supplies, constrained the business response to new market opportunities. Reducing government intervention was not sufficient to spur sustained growth. Other improvements in the institutional framework were necessary, not least of which was strengthening the government's own capacity to design and implement public sector interventions necessary to support decentralised market activities. In general the shift in management of the economy towards market orientation and private sector development eased the otherwise tight control system and generated initial growth that way. However, the growth recovery could not be sustained as it soon came up against an institutional framework which was inappropriate for a market economy and private sector development. Institutional reforms were needed. In this context, the emphasis of the Third Phase Government on institutional reforms is well placed.

The low growth rate for total GDP was associated with the poor performance of the largest sector, agriculture, which grew at an average rate of only 2.8 percent during the 1995-1998 period, while tourism and mining sectors recorded the highest real GDP growth rate (averaging at 18.8 percent and 18.1 percent). Annual growth in GDP of less than 3 percent implies that per capita output levels are stagnating. Performance during the Third Phase Government has been just above that level. In the longer term, significantly higher growth will have to be achieved if national development goals are to be attained.

The economic philosophy underlying structural adjustment reforms is that if the economy is allowed to respond to market stimulus, in an environment of reasonable macroeconomic stability, in which government concentrates on provision of basic social services and infrastructure, the economy can be expected to achieve its growth potential. However, even if that approach to policy is valid, it gives no guidance as to the level of Tanzanian growth potential.

The Long Term Development Vision 2025 (Planning Commission) suggests that the country should aspire to an 8 percent growth rate - a vision of Tanzania as an economic tiger. But the Tanzanian economy has never grown at anything like that rate. Even in the buoyant growth period following Independence (1961-67), growth was only around 6 percent per annum. Experience of high growth in the East Asian economies in the last thirty years suggests that achieving 8 percent growth may be possible, but only under stringent conditions. These might include a sustained high rate of savings and investment to expand capacity, utilising existing capacity more effectively, the provision of strong incentives and other required support for export promotion, backed up by innovative learning from the experience of others and from our own past experience.

Economic activity is limited by a number of basic macroeconomic constraints, which are discussed below under the following headings:

(a) Agricultural growth

(b) Growth in foreign exchange earnings
(c) Capital formation
(d) Human and institutional development

Agricultural growth

The importance of agriculture
The economy is still heavily dependent on agriculture and on informal economic activities, and the growth in such activities, therefore, has a large influence on the overall growth rate. Agriculture is the most important sector in terms of contribution to GDP, exports and employment. In 1998 the agricultural sector contributed about 50 percent to GDP, 70-80 percent to total employment and 55 percent of the country's foreign exchange. It is the source of income for the majority of the population, and therefore its performance is a critical determinant of welfare. Given the fact that many services and processing activities are directly dependent on agriculture, significantly more than half of GDP growth is linked to agricultural growth.

Monetary activities are estimated to contribute around 56 percent of the agricultural GDP, compared with 44 percent coming from subsistence production. The non-monetary agricultural GDP is large because most farmers are small scale farmers producing part of their output for household use or local unrecorded trade. According to the 1994/95 agricultural census, over 3.9 million households were involved in small scale farming with an average farm size of 0.9 hectares. Large scale farming accounted for only 14 percent of agricultural output.

In the early stages of development high rates of growth in agriculture are necessary as a basis for achieving growth in other sectors. Surplus generated in agriculture is instrumental in transforming the economy. However, even in highly successful economies, trend growth in agricultural output of more than 5-6 percent has rarely been achieved.

Agriculture remains important enough that it is not possible for the economy as a whole to achieve targeted growth rates without a positive performance from the sector. Sustained agricultural growth somewhat above the population growth rate (say around 3.5 percent per annum, if a conservative estimate is adopted, or 5-6 percent if a more desirable target is aimed at) is needed to ensure good growth performance for the economy as a whole. Agricultural growth rates at that level and higher have been associated with the early stages of economic success in a number of Asian economies.

Agricultural growth in historical perspective
This section places the current situation of Tanzanian agriculture in

historical perspective. Experience from the colonial period is of interest, as the liberalisation measures of recent years have in many ways replicated colonial policies by concentrating on agricultural exports. Such policies are based on the assumption that Tanzania has a comparative advantage as an agricultural exporter in today's global economy.

Tanganyika, which was administered by the British as a League of Nations and then a UN Trust for four decades, operated as a mixed model of African smallholder and non-African owned large scale agriculture.[1] Sisal, at independence the largest export, was almost entirely a plantation crop. Coffee production was roughly evenly divided between African smallholders and non-African owned large farms. Cotton was a smallholder crop. Non-African farmers and plantation companies produced minor exports, such as tobacco and tea, and Africans supplied hides and skins and a number of other minor export items. At the end of the colonial period, exports were roughly evenly divided between African and non-African producers.[2]

Earlier experience has shown that the consequences of agricultural export development depend not only on the nature of trade specialisation, but also on the mode and organisation of production. The historical case for the positive impact of agricultural export trade rests largely on the performance and impact of smallholder export agriculture. Smallholder agricultural exports experienced periods of dynamic growth. The growth of coffee production in Kagera, Kilimanjaro and the Southern Highlands and of cotton, particularly in the western zone, provided a basis for relatively prosperous rural communities in the decades prior to Independence. Following Independence, during the period 1960/62-1967, there was a sustained burst of growth in Tanzanian export crop production with lively rates of growth in the established major crops, coffee and cotton, and very high rates of what had been minor crops, such as cashews and tobacco.

The record of dynamic expansion provides good *prima facie* evidence of the potential of smallholder farming to become part of the global economy. The impact of increased export production on farming communities was very positive - funding improved housing, living standards, and education. Smallholder export farming systems began to support a broad middle-class of prosperous farmers, and it was from these areas that a disproportionate number of the future educated elite was recruited. This was surely a far superior way of integrating into the international economy than as wage labourers, as in the Kenya White Highlands or the Tanganyika sisal estates. Given the evidence of the positive impact of these developments in the past, what questions can be raised about this mode of development for the future? One set of issues relates to the limits of smallholder agricultural export growth.

There are four main areas to consider when looking at the constraints on agricultural export growth:

(a) Geographical limits: The areas of concentrated high-income export crop farming have been geographically limited, particularly to fertile highland areas suitable for tree crop cultivation. There are large populated areas of Tanzania, which do not share in such opportunities, where, for example, annual export crops compete with food production in low yield rain-fed farming systems. This limits the potential contribution to national growth and opens up the prospect of regional inequality.

(b) Limits on productivity growth: The dynamic growth in export crops has typically resulted from the introduction of new higher value crops, rather than from the increased productivity of those crops within the existing farming system. Once new crops have reached their geographical limit, output growth is constrained by the inability to increase yields.

(c) Limits resulting from competition with food crops: At the initial stages of export crop production, either because of the lack of direct competition with food production, or because of the economic benefits gained from increased specialisation, export production was not tightly constrained by competition with food crops. As Tanzania has become more densely populated and urbanised, food crop production for the local market (including cross-border trade) has become an option that has increased the price-supply elasticity of some export crops (e.g. competition of rice with cotton).[3] This situation is likely to be more intense with the dynamic growth of non-agricultural activities such as mining and tourism.

(d) Demand limits in international markets: The case against specialisation in primary commodity exports because of the presumed limitations of demand has some force at the global level, both when considering demand for primary commodities in general and demand for most individual primary commodities. It carries less weight when applied to particular countries; Tanzania is a price taker in almost all commodity markets.[4] Even in a declining market it may be possible to increase revenues by increasing market share, particularly if one is a relatively low cost producer.[5] It seems likely that higher rates of supply growth would have generated more or less commensurate increases in revenues in most crops.

Over the long haul, however, the problems of smallholders have not derived so much from conditions in international markets (e.g. negative movements in international terms of trade, although those have occurred), as from internal marketing arrangements and macroeconomic policies which have shifted the internal terms of trade against exporters. Thus the vulnerability of small farmers has not been so much to the vagaries of the global economy as to the policies of colonial and national governments.[6]

Analysis of the historical record suggests that:

(a) With favourable incentives, producing export crops for global markets can contribute to growth in export earnings.
(b) It is necessary to develop the capacity for monitoring developments in the world market, to make appropriate responses to changing demands.
(c) Introduction of new crops of high market value can be an effective way of increasing the performance of an existing farming system.
(d) Agricultural performance can be improved by selectively growing appropriate crops in locations that are best suited for them.
(e) Expansion of agricultural exports will not by itself sustain the growth in total export earnings required to underwrite sustained expansion in per capita incomes over the longer term.

The longer term transformation of agriculture and growth in the incomes of farm households will require a dramatic increase in labour productivity in the sector. However, the diverse nature of the sector means that this will not be achieved by one major innovation, but will require many changes appropriate to particular cropping systems, local soils and climatic conditions. Appropriate technical changes are likely to vary, for example, from the highly intensive cropping systems of the fertile highland areas, where land is scarce, production focuses on tree crops and yields per hectare are already high, to the more extensive agriculture of the lowland areas planted to annual crops. One implication of these realities is that agricultural transformation will rely on efforts made at the regional and local levels.

Current performance

The sector's performance is summarised in Table 2.

Agricultural output fluctuates from year to year, largely in response to climate. Drought in 1992 and 1994 and drought in the first half of 1997/98 followed by the El Niño rains in the second half of the year resulted in poor performances in each of those years. On the other hand, 1990 and 1995 experienced good harvests, with growth of more than 5 percent. Performance over the period 1987-91 suggested that reform may have had a strong impact in stimulating higher growth, but in the period since 1991 only two years (1995 and 1996) have seen positive per capita agricultural growth.

Table 2: Performance of Agricultural Sector in Tanzania, 1987-1998 (1992 prices)

Year	Ag. GDP Growth	Share in Total GDP	Ag. Export Growth	Exports Value US$ mil.	Share in Total Export Earnings
1987	-	48.7	-23.1	201.24	58.0
1988	2.2	47.7	11.4	224.25	60.3
1989	3.9	48.3	-2.3	212.78	56.2
1990	5.5	47.9	-8.7	201.4	50.1
1991	3.6	48.3	0.7	233.3	55.6
1992	1.2	48.0	16.7	188.3	58.7
1993	3.1	49.3	9.0	162.2	58.3
1994	2.1	49.6	31.5	220.16	64.9
1995	5.8	50.7	13.9	253.05	56.2
1996	3.9	50.6	16.6	276.59	58.7
1997	2.5	50.1	-19.4	228.04	50.2
1998	1.9	49.4	-4.1	189.32	51.1

Source: National Accounts, Hali ya Uchumi, Bank of Tanzania: Economic and Operation Report (various issues) and Tanzanian Economic Trends (1995).

Note: The agricultural sector has been subject to an active reform programme, including the removal of most controls, such as restrictions on the marketing and transportation of food grains (abolished in 1989), freeing of producer prices (between 1991/92-1993/94), and opening up the marketing of major traditional crops to private traders.

Table 3: Production of Main Export Crops (thousand metric tonnes)

Export Crop	1993/1994	1994/1995	1995/1996	1996/1997	Peak Production Period	Peak Production Amount
Coffee	48.5	43.5	52.0	41.0	1980/81	66.6
Cotton	48.4	44.5	84.2	84.5	1996/97	84.5
Tea	22.4	24.8	25.0	24.0	1997/98	25.5
Cashew	46.6	63.4	82.0	63.0	1973/74	143.3
Tobacco	24.0	22.4	28.0	35.4	1997/98	52.0
Sisal	30.5	25.5	23.0	30.0	1964	230.0

Source: Respective marketing Boards and Authorities as reported in BoT (1999).

Severe weather conditions are often the cause of bad harvests. Historically the pattern has been for two or three difficult years in each decade. Target performance, therefore, should be defined in terms of the trend, averaging good years with bad. In those terms, the performance of agriculture since the introduction of the ERP has been disappointing.

While some export crops have been revived, and agriculture has performed well in providing the bulk of the food consumed in Tanzania, the aggregate data give little evidence to suggest a decisive improvement in the long term trend in agricultural growth as compared to the pre-reform years. Although agriculture is not so burdened by the high costs of state marketing monopolies, the competitive network of commercial traders is still weak. While the system is handling established commodities well, it is still limited in relation to the more sophisticated role of spreading new crops, seeds and techniques.

Table 4: Growth Rates of Agriculture

	1985 – 1990	1990 – 1998	1985 – 1998
Main Food Crops:			
Maize	2.0	2.7	2.4
Paddy	21.7	4.4	10.7
Wheat	9.6	0.6	4.0
Millet/ Sorghum	5.5	5.1	0.9
Cassava	9.8	0.2	3.8
Beans	0.3	2.3	1.6
Subtotal	**4.3**	**3.0**	**3.5**
Other food Crops	3.0	2.8	2.9
Export Crops:			
Seed Cotton	11.6	1.9	5.5
Green Tea	3.8	3.3	3.5
Coffee	4.2	-7.3	-3.0
Sisal	2.4	-2.3	-0.5
Tobacco	-3.4	21.8	11.4
Cashewnuts	-12.3	24.8	8.9
Total Agriculture	**3.7**	**3.5**	**3.5**

Source: National Bureau of Statistics (1999)

Food production and food policy

With the exception of wheat and rice, in most years Tanzania is substantially self-sufficient in food staples, only having to import maize during years of bad harvests. One of the more successful aspects of the reform process has been the shift from a controlled market for the main staples, served by the National Milling Corporation at great cost to the national budget, to an unsubsidised competitive system. Malnutrition, which remains a serious problem, is mainly due to inadequate food supplies and income at the household level, rather than market scarcity.

Table 5: Production of Major Food Crops (thousand metric tonnes)

Crop	1993/ 1994	1994/ 1995	1995/ 1996	1996/ 1997	1997/ 1998	Peak Prod'n Period	Amt.
Maize	2159.0	2567.0	2638.0	1835.0	2750.0	1998/89	3125.0
Paddy	614.0	723.0	681.3	550.8	810.8	1997/98	810.8
Wheat	59.4	75.0	61.0	78.0	111.0	1989/90	106.0
Pulses	186.7	374.0	384.0	374.0	453.0	1997/98	453.0
Banana	834.0	651.0	631.0	603.0	892.0	1997/98	892.0
Cassava	1415.0	1492.0	1478.0	1426.0	1528.0	1991/92	1778.0
Potatoes	277.0	451.0	446.0	480.0	394.0	1989/90	996.1
Sorghum	478.0	839.0	1250.0	498.5	868.0	1995/96	1250.0
Total	5808.1	6919.0	7365.0	5989.0	7523.0		

Source: Ministry of Agriculture as reported in BoT (1999)

Over the long term, the growth in food production, which has been more or less in line with population growth, has been the most successful aspect of Tanzanian agriculture. The trend growth in total food production has matched population growth. Also there has been a shift in the composition of food output to meet changing demand (e.g. the relatively high growth in paddy production), and the needs of the fast growing urban population. The growth in production of food for the market means that the traditional distinction between cash crops and food crops has blurred, as many farmers now derive their main cash income from the sale of food crops.

National Food Security Policy faces a basic dilemma. While Tanzania is able to supply itself with much of its food during an average year and to export food surpluses to neighbouring countries, it does not necessarily make economic sense to pursue national food security through self-sufficiency, because of wide fluctuations in food production due to weather. For example, staples production is estimated to have declined from 7,365 metric tonnes in 1995/96 to 5,989 metric tonnes in 1996/97. As shortfalls are unpredictable before the season begins, the reserve stocks which have to be carried in good years to ensure self-sufficiency in bad years can be unduly expensive, particularly if they are required to cover the needs of two successive weak harvests (as has happened).

High transport costs prevent Tanzania from becoming a substantial exporter of staples to overseas markets (i.e. it would not be economic to aim for surplus production for export, so that the impact of output fluctuations on the domestic market could be cushioned by adjustments in exports).

Realistically, therefore, in the short run it makes economic sense to continue to import to deal with years of serious shortfalls in domestic supply. For this purpose, the maintenance of an effective early warning system, to identify potential supply failure as early as possible, is critically important. In the medium to longer term, it will be necessary to develop robust crop varieties (of drought resistant seeds) and enhance investments in irrigation.

Prospects for future growth
There have been enough positive aspects in the performance of the agricultural sector to validate the market based reforms. The end of state purchasing monopolies and the ready supply of goods in markets improved the environment for smallholders. The New Agricultural and Livestock Policy (ALP) adopted in 1997 reiterated government support for the liberalised policy regime, which had been developed over the previous decade. Perhaps equally important over the long term may be the introduction of a New Land Policy (NLP), 1995, which has been translated into legislation, and is intended to improve the institutional environment within which farmers operate. The long term record is that smallholder farming systems respond to market opportunities and price stimulus, both positively and negatively. Within this sector there has been a surprising degree of spontaneous innovation, perhaps most evident in the development of new food crops (fruits and vegetables) to supply the fast growing urban market.

With a continuation of the liberal marketing policies and a stable macroeconomic environment, some degree of continuing progress may be expected. However, part of the growth achieved in such crops as cotton and cashew following reform may prove to be a one-off response to improved market conditions. Perhaps the most difficult challenge facing the Third Phase Government will be to find means of increasing underlying productivity growth in the agricultural sector.

To achieve sustained annual growth in the economy of 8 percent, agricultural growth needs to be raised from its trend level 2-3 percent to at least 3.5 percent (for a conservative projection or 5-6 percent for a more desirable target). In its election manifesto in 1995 the ruling party, CCM, set itself the task of promoting the modernisation of agriculture, livestock and fisheries, and set out a number of objectives:

(a)   expansion of fertiliser use;
(b)   greater use of ploughs and oxcarts;
(c)   promote acquisition of tractors;
(d)   consolidate and develop marketing;
(e)   strengthen research and extension services;

(f)   use progressive farmers to teach other farmers;
(g)   strengthen and enhance the agricultural Input Trust Fund;
(h)   enhance small scale irrigation;
(i)   rehabilitate and construct dips, dams and develop reliable grazing;
(j)   address problems of small fishermen by increasing provision of nets, boats and other equipment; and
(k)   promote large scale deep sea fishing, based on joint ventures.

As a list of possible developments that could contribute to acceleration in agricultural growth, this one makes reasonable sense. However, what is less clear is how the government can ensure that such developments take place. General exhortations to farmers are likely to have little effect. Rather, farmers require economically viable solutions, to specific problems, which take into account their severe resource constraints.

The outlook is not particularly good. The impact of policy on the agricultural sector in the 1960s and 1970s was largely negative, particularly in disrupting marketing channels and depressing the real terms of trade facing farmers. At the present time, research and extension capacity is weak and many aspects of agriculture are not well understood. This is partly because local variations in cropping systems and natural conditions are often not recorded and can, therefore, be misinterpreted.[7] The record of donor funded programmes in agriculture has been at best unimpressive. Although poor performance in the pre-reform period may, in part, be attributed to the poor macroeconomic environment. There has also been persistent weakness in project design (a well established tradition going back to colonial groundnut schemes).

However, even if the overall record of donor intervention is unimpressive, there have been some recent successes from which lessons can be drawn. For example, the Heifer Trust Scheme, implemented with notable success in Kagera, Tanga, Iringa, Mbeya and Mara. This scheme, with the participation of local farmers, has brought about gradual improvements in the productivity of these regions through the promotion of appropriate innovation.

The government and donors have initiated a number of new programmes aimed at raising productivity, including:

(a)   The Agriculture Input Trust Fund, which was established in 1995/96. The funds are used to import and distribute farm inputs. Some 117 businessmen had borrowed Tshs 1,085 million by 1997. And in 1998 about Tshs 979.5 million was issued as loans. Despite this facility, input supplies are still reported to fall significantly short of technical estimates of requirements.

(b) Efforts have been made to revive extension work. The National Agricultural Extension Programme (NAEP II) and the Southern Highlands Extension and Rural Financial Services (SHERSP) are reported to have trained a total of 2000 farmers in 1997, up from 1450 farmers in 1996. About 4,227,972 cattle were vaccinated against tick borne diseases and 1015 cattle against pneumonia. In 1998 the two programmes continued to offer training to extension officers, providing equipment and building staff quarters for extension officers. A total of 2,372 farmers were trained in agricultural centres, and some 1140 farmers went on study tours, while about 110,890 farmers received training on their farms. However, although this effort was significant, it touched only a tiny proportion of farmers.

(c) The National Agriculture and Livestock Research Project (NALRP) and the Tanzania Agriculture Research Project (TARPII) have been funded to undertake research in such areas as farming systems, agroforestry, animal traction and the use of grass legume varieties for soil conservation in drought stricken areas.

These efforts represent fairly traditional approaches to public intervention in the agricultural sector, which have not had a great impact on agricultural performance. However, in the past, sharp changes in policy and institutional arrangements, and discontinuities in institutions and personnel, which disrupted the learning process, undermined agricultural development efforts. What may be required is a sustained, longer term effort to increase the knowledge base required for the design of more effective interventions. Agricultural research, careful analysis of the sources of growth in those sub-sectors which have performed well in recent years, and, more careful monitoring of the performance of existing projects should eventually yield results. Perhaps too little has been learnt from past successes and failures.

At this stage of Tanzanian agricultural development, in the absence of a solid agricultural research base, potentially the most critical government intervention in support of agriculture could come from the improvement of Tanzania's physical infrastructure and the development of an effective transport system. In Tanzania, areas of high potential agricultural land are widely dispersed. This makes the sector particularly vulnerable to the high costs of transport, unreliable long distance transport and the limited availability of all-weather feeder roads. As a result of poor infrastructure, potentially high food producing areas in south-western Tanzania often find they are isolated from Dar es Salaam and other food deficit areas. However, it is hoped that government decentralisation and increases in the allocation of development funds at the district level will lead to improvements in local roads and transport systems, and that investments in infrastructure will become more responsive to local farmers needs.

The priority government and donors give to agriculture is sometimes measured by the public investment allocated to agriculture. This has been, and remains low, but looking only at direct investments in the sector can be misleading. A key requirement for small farmers is access to low cost, all-weather communications. In the coming period the challenge will be to link up high potential areas more effectively to the national transport grid, and to stimulate production throughout the country, by connecting local production areas to the trunk system through all-weather feeder roads. Perhaps the most revealing index of the government and donor commitment to agricultural development will be the priority given to developing the trunk, district and feeder road system serving farmers.

A potential source of on-farm productivity improvement is through the spread of new crops, and new seeds and varieties of existing crops, which should be a major focus of research and extension. Past periods of dynamic expansion in Tanzanian agriculture have been associated with the rapid spread of new crops (e.g. in the early 1960s). In more recent years the fast growth of horticultural products, such as flowers, has originated from new entrants into a new area. However, while a strengthened research and extension service can play its role in this regard, the spread of innovations through the commercial distribution system and informal channels are likely to be even more important.[8] The key policy need is to accommodate and encourage existing commercial distributors and new entrants.

There has been a good deal of discussion regarding the need for credit and rural micro-finance. The past record of development finance in agriculture is riddled with many difficulties. Lessons should be drawn from those experiences in a systematic way. In relation to agricultural credit, at least two needs should be distinguished:

(a) The need for short term crop finance, both to the farmer and the trader, in order to finance input supply and crop trade. This has always been an important call on the resources of the Tanzanian financial system, both in the era of the parastatal trading system and in earlier days, and will continue to be in the future. If properly organised, this is a relatively safe form of lending, as it is self-liquidating over the crop season. However, availability of such finance has been adversely affected by the tribulations of the banking system, and weaknesses in the crop marketing system. Improved access will depend on the more effective functioning of both in the future.

(b) The second need is for development finance to support investments to improve on-farm productivity. This is a more problematic area. There is an underlying problem regarding medium term lending to agriculture. Most smallholder farmers have little capital, so that even limited borrowing would result in a high debt equity ratio. Agriculture is inherently risky, and it is does not make good sense for a farmer to get into debt unless there are assured prospects that the application of additional capital will bring commensurate productivity increases. Such prospects may exist, for example, where a farmer has the possibility of introducing a new high-value crop, but will depend on the flow of knowledge to the farmer regarding options to improve incomes.

Community level investments in infrastructure (e.g. dams, dips, and rural roads) should be encouraged in order to increase productivity and reduce risk. The complementarity between investments by individuals and community level investments needs to be recognised in order that arrangements can be made to tap it effectively.

Foreign exchange earnings

The importance of exports
Tanzania is heavily dependent on imports, and the level of economic activity is constrained by the rate of growth in import capacity. Efforts to promote import substitution in the 1970s did little to reduce import dependence, as the new industries were dependent on imported inputs, the shortage of which held down capacity utilisation. Imports either have to be paid for from foreign exchange earnings (i.e. commodity exports and invisible earnings), or from foreign capital in-flows (grants, loans and investments). While capital in-flows may play a part in financing imports, in the past Tanzania has been too heavily dependent on official external finance, and it would be imprudent to an ever increasing in-flow. Tanzania must export more to sustain higher growth.

Globalisation and future development
The emphasis on the need for more buoyant exports is based on the view that sustained import expansion requires sustained growth in export earnings. And, indeed, most successful growth performances in recent decades have been firmly based on export led growth. However, there has also been a recurring theme in the development literature regarding the dangers of external dependence.

Currently, there is a good deal of international discussion of globalisation and its implications for development. In certain key respects, the phenomenon of globalisation is not particularly new in its impact on peripheral economies. Throughout its colonial history, the Tanganyikan economy was subject to the dominant metropolitan influences of the German and then the British Empires. Growth was led by production for the international market. Sisal, the largest export, had been introduced quite explicitly to meet German naval requirements. At Independence, the economy was heavily dependent on imports to meet its requirements for manufactured goods and even moderately sophisticated technology, and the financial sector was totally under international ownership.

The transnational corporation was not unknown to the colonial economy. The great colonial trading companies operated between and across continents, and had often played a crucial role in shaping political developments. The impact of the global economy was a central theme in the radical literature on the East African economies.[9] Many of the issues to be confronted in relation to current day globalisation are not dissimilar to problems addressed in the past. The specific developments in the past decades that have given rise to much debate on globalisation are:

(a) the increased mobility in the location of industrial production, with the resulting shift of much industrial activity from the established centres in the industrial economies;

(b) the greatly increased importance of international financial markets, with the resulting limitations on the capacity of national governments to pursue independent monetary and foreign exchange policies;

(c) the increase in the size and cosmopolitan character of the large corporations, rendering them less susceptible to control by their home authorities;

(d) the demise of the Soviet bloc, and the emergence of an unchallenged hegemony of free-market economics, underwritten by a system of multilateral agreements and organisations geared to promote the operation of all aspects of international finance and trade on free-market principles; and

(e) with the attempts to integrate the previous Soviet bloc into the international market, and the widespread adoption of liberal trade and foreign exchange policies by almost all developing economies, there is now an almost universal aspiration to participate in the global economy.

For peripheral economies, the significance of globalisation over the past three decades has varied enormously. The benefits that could accrue to successful participation in the global economy were well illustrated by the success of the East Asian economies; the growth of their industrial exports and the increased mobility of capital resulted in extraordinarily high growth for a generation.

For Africa, however, the story of the past generation has been quite different. Africa has experienced marginalisation rather than globalisation. The African continent is now of less economic interest to the rest of the world, as a market, a source of commodities, or for investment than during the colonial period. Africa is of little consequence in the main commercial centres; this contrasts with East Asia - when it gets economic pneumonia, at least the northern financial markets get the 'flu'. Even in relation to the continent's traditional role as a producer of primary commodities, the relative importance of Africa in world trade has declined. And Africa has not participated significantly in the global shift in industrial production away from Europe and North America. It has not featured in the internationalisation of equity markets and, compared with a number of Asian countries, its participation in the market for migrant labour has been minor. There was greater interest shown at the end of the 1960s by international business in investment in East Africa than subsequently. In relation to international capital movements, the only sense in which there has been increased globalisation has been through increasing dependence on foreign aid, particularly during the 1970s.

For those who are suspicious of globalisation, the marginalisation of Africa might be a source of satisfaction if it was the result of a successful alternative - a more self-reliant strategy. However, this is far from the case. The current condition has either emerged from the failure of attempts at more autonomous development (as in the case of Tanzania), or from weak performances in economies which attempted to integrate into the international economy (a possible interpretation of the Kenya experience). Moreover, many economies have been implementing structural adjustment programmes for more than a decade, which have aimed to boost foreign trade and investment - the limited success in accelerating integration in the global economy has been at variance with the hopes held out by those promoting structural adjustment.

In considering the consequences of the marginalisation of Africa in relation to globalisation, to be excluded from the process might be considered worse than being included in a disadvantaged fashion. If there is only one game in town (i.e. free-trade), that is the game that has to be played. Therefore a key task for economic policy must be to increase participation in the global economy. Tanzania will need to focus on its supply capacity in order to tap the opportunities offered by a liberalising regional and international regime (Atkinson, 1999).[10] Of course, a related set of questions concern strategies to maximise the benefits and minimise the costs of such participation, but there is little point in raising alarm about the dangers of globalisation when it is not even clear that Tanzania is a participant in the globalisation process.

Participation in global markets implies striving to attain international competitiveness. That requires a sound macroeconomic framework, development of technical capabilities to reduce costs and improve product quality and building the capacity to generate new products and penetrate new markets. Policy makers will need to give priority to enhancing the capacity to understand developments in the world economy and the capacity to respond rationally to those developments.

Traditional exports
While some traditional exports have responded to the stimulus of economic reform, the picture is quite mixed.

Table 6: Traditional Export Crops

Export crop	1970	1973	1976	1983	1989	1993	1996	1998	Peak prod'n	
									Year	Amt.
Coffee	44.6	47.0	55.4	50.7	50.4	58.6	64.0	53.6	1990	87.1
Cotton	70.0	76.7	42.0	39.8	31.7	61.2	89.7	36.0	1996	89.7
Tea	8.5	12.8	13.0	16.6	9.5	19.8	24.7	22.7	1996	24.7
Cashews	111.4	125.3	83.4	17.2	23.6	32.2	121.2	140.4	1998	140.4
Tobacco	11.0	13.0	18.7	10.5	17.8	10.6	24.0	12.7	1981	35.2
Sisal	202.0	155.4	118.0	26.8	15.1	5.0	7.6	10.9	1970	202.0

Source: Respective marketing boards and authorities as reported in BoT (1999).

Cotton production has had the most significant success in recovery among traditional export crops in response to economic reforms. Exports had fallen to 22 thousand tonnes in 1985 from a peak volume of 76 thousand tonnes in 1971. A sustained expansion led to exports of 90 thousand tonnes in 1996 - an all time peak. The recent decline can be partly attributed to the climatic cycle and failures in market management.

Cashewnut export has also been a success of the reform process. Exports had collapsed from a peak of 145 thousand tonnes in 1974 to 6.5 thousand tonnes in 1990. Since then there has been an impressive revival, mainly in response to liberalised marketing arrangements, with exports approaching their earlier peak.

Coffee production has fluctuated around a flat trend for three decades; it did not decline as badly as many other crops during the period of economic crisis, but has not expanded since the initiation of reforms. Tea, which had declined during the crisis years (but not as catastrophically as sisal and cashews), came back strongly in 1990, but has since been on a production plateau. Tobacco exports, which had continued to expand during the early 1980s, have since stagnated.

The performance of sisal has been miserable. Thirty-five years ago sisal was the major Tanzanian export, accounting for around two-fifths of total export earnings. The impact of nationalisation and the underlying difficulties in the world hard-fibre market led to the secular decline of the industry. By 1990, exports had fallen to three thousand tonnes, less than 2 percent of levels in 1970. There has been some recovery since, but exports are still only around 5 percent the peak achieved in the mid-1960s.

Interpretation of the long term performance of traditional exports during the Third Phase Government is difficult because they remain subject to wide cyclical fluctuations. During 1997/98, earnings from agricultural exports declined by 20.6 percent to US $325.5 million from US $410.1 million recorded in 1996/97. This was caused by both volume and price factors. Coffee, cotton and cashewnuts recorded lower export receipts mainly due to declining volumes; the result of bad weather in the 1996/97 and 1997/98 crop seasons. Sisal and tobacco registered declines in both volumes and unit export prices. Tea was the only crop that registered higher export earnings because of the surge in its price as well as an increase in export quantum.

Food exports
One policy issue that needs more systematic treatment relates to cross-border agricultural trade. Tanzania has long been a net food exporter to Eastern Africa - this was already true in the days of the East African Community. Much of the trade is unrecorded in official statistics, partly because policy has often discouraged such trade, in some cases making it illegal (in August 1999 large shipments of maize were being seized at the Kenya border, because informal sales of maize were illegal, according to the regional authorities). If all such exports were fully recorded, Tanzanian export performance would appear significantly more positive.

Official ambivalence to the food trade has a long history. In the colonial period, paternalistic by-laws even restricted inter-district trade, as a food security measure, and some of the continuing ambivalence regarding cross-border trade may reflect a continuing assumption that national food security is best protected by preventing the out-flow of food. There is little merit in such a view. It is more likely that national food security will be higher if Tanzania develops a substantial cross-border export trade in foodstuffs, as an outlet for surplus food production would encourage farmers to produce higher levels of output.[11] The wish to protect the food consumer at the expense of farmers may be one hidden objective, but apart from the negative distributional implications of such an approach, it is also likely to be counter-productive, discouraging food production. It should also be noted that given the costly internal transport system, and the location of food surplus areas, it may make good sense to export food to markets in neighbouring countries at the same time as supplying deficit areas (e.g. Dar es Salaam) by importing.

There has been a tendency to emphasise the virtues of continuing with traditional export crop production rather than shifting to food production. Official interventions from time to time have even forbidden farmers from uprooting coffee, despite their judgement that it makes better economic sense to shift to food production. This may be partly motivated by the obsolete vocabulary that distinguishes food (subsistence) crops from export (cash) crops, which confuses a number of issues.

From the farmers point of view cash derived from food crop sales, now a considerable part of cash transactions, is no different from cash derived from export crops. And export income derived from cross-border trade is the same as export income earned overseas, so that even if official policy is biased towards export production, there is no reason why that should not include exports to neighbouring countries. Indeed, it makes little economic or moral sense to emphasise the virtues of selling coffee overseas whilst discouraging the sale of maize or beans to neighbouring countries.

Non-traditional exports
Given the apparent constraints on the output of traditional exports, diversification into new exports has been a recurring stated objective of the Tanzanian government. However, what little success was achieved in diversification in the 1960s and 1970s was eroded in the years of crisis in the early 1980s, as the crisis in production affected exports along with all other activities, and sharp increases in the real effective exchange rate discouraged exporters. During the Second and Third Phase Governments there has been some success in diversifying foreign exchange earnings - not yet sustained enough to herald an era of export led growth, but nevertheless a pointer to future possibilities.

Table 7: Compound Growth Rates (%) of Non-Traditional Exports 1961 -1997

	1961-76*	1976-81	1981-86	1986-97
Non Traditional Exports	11	10	-18	17
Merchandise, of which:	7	18	-29	24
Petroleum Products	1	-5	-3	68
Minerals	6	21	-70	21
Manufactured	8	9	-42	39
Others	2	71	-19	18
Services, of which:	15	5	-11	15
Tourism	-2	10	-1	31

Source: URT Economic Surveys (various) * Note: For petroleum products, minerals and tourism the periods are 1967-76, 1961-1976 and 1970-1976 respectively.

Potential dynamic comparative advantage

Apart from the traditional export crops, the possible sources of foreign exchange earnings can be considered under three main headings; tourism, mining and industrial export processing. The possibility of generating significant foreign exchange from labour remittances (as a number of Asian and Latin American countries did in the past) does not, at this point, seem great.

Mineral exports

Tanzania's mining potential has hardly been developed, but now provides the best medium term prospect for rapid export growth. Numerous issues of public policy need to be addressed in relation to both the artisanal and the large scale sectors.[12] The licensing and taxation of mining and negotiation with multinationals is a highly complex area, in relation to which Tanzanian experience is limited.[13] There has been some comment that the tax/royalty package given to the new large scale mining concessions have been too generous, leaving too little of the value added in the country. On the other hand, it might have been appropriate to provide special incentives to pioneer developments. This study does not offer any conclusion on that issue, but merely notes that if the mining sector is going to grow as large as current estimates suggest, study of the taxation and financial arrangements for future development should have high priority.

The mining sector grew rapidly during the first three years of the Third Phase Government with the real GDP of the mining sector growing at 18 percent per annum, during the 1996-1998 years. This acceleration in growth was partly a result of reform and liberalisation measures allowing for the greater role of the private sector. Measures taken by the government included encouragement of new investors, liberalisation of the sector, putting in place an attractive fiscal regime and the formulation of the Mineral Policy and Mining Development Strategy of Tanzania in 1997. That policy includes a legal and regulatory framework that seeks to provide clearer and simpler procedures for the granting, sale and transfer of mining rights. The role of the private sector is emphasised. The future role of the government in the mining sector will be to concentrate on developing an enabling environment and facilitating institutional, legal and infrastructure support to the sector.

There has been an increase in private sector participation, as the number of mineral prospecting and mining licences issued increased from 235 in 1996 to 375 and 389 in 1997 and 1998, respectively. About 80 percent of the mineral rights licences were issued to local miners, while the rest were to foreign investors. More than 60 percent of the licensed companies are undertaking mining activities in the Lake zone.

Table 8: Performance of Mining Sector in Tanzania: 1987-1998

Year	Mining GDP Growth	Share in Total GDP	Mineral Export Growth	Share in Total Exports	Share in NT Exports
1987	-	0.8	-	-	-
1988	-1.3	0.8	-	-	-
1989	13.0	0.8	-	-	-
1990	16.5	0.9	-		-
1991	11.7	1.0	-	11.5	25.9
1992	7.7	1.1	-1.9	10.2	24.6
1993	8.2	1.1	69.1	15.7	37.7
1994	156.0	1.3	-56.5	5.8	16.4
1995	11.7	1.4	49.6	6.6	15.0
1996	9.7	1.5	12.2	6.6	16.0
1997	17.1	1.7	84.3	12.9	25.9
1998	27.4	2.0	11.0	15.2	31.2

Source: Economic Survey (various) and BoT (1999)

Despite recent growth, the share of the sector in GDP is still small (less than 2 percent according to official estimates, although possibly more given the unrecorded trade). The sector's share in exports is more important; by 1998 minerals accounted for 15 percent of exports and for 31 percent of non-traditional exports. Gold and diamonds contributed about 63.9 percent of the sector's exports and gemstones about 36 percent.

The most important potential for future export growth over the medium term relates to gold. Gold exports increased to 427 kilograms in 1998, from 232 kilograms in 1997. In 1998 foreign companies initiated projects which are expected to result in an investment of some US $360 million in gold mining. Following the opening of new mines it is estimated that about 5,400 kilograms of gold, worth around US $50 million, could be exported in the near future, with medium term prospects of exports very much higher than that. Prospects may be affected by negative price movements. In recent years the gold price has proved as volatile as most other primary commodities. The price of gold declined from an average of US $385 per ounce in 1994 to an average of US $282 per ounce in the early months of 1999. However, the large deposits being developed are low cost and should remain viable even at the low prices recently experienced.

The mining industry consists of two sub-sectors - the larger scale mines, involving foreign investment, and a large amount of small scale artisanal activity. Artisanal mining involves tens of thousands of workers; estimates have suggested that as many as 500,000 workers are involved in the industry.

The output of the artisanal sector is uncertain because much of the output enters informal trading channels.

Longer term implications of mining development
The mining boom which is predicted in official estimates of potential deposits and possible output growth could have profound implications for the Tanzanian economy in four to five years time - reducing the dependence on aid, easing budgetary constraints and generating much faster growth in export earnings. Such developments could change the basic characteristics of the economy. But, while this presents a much brighter prospect for Tanzanian economic growth, such developments are not without risk. If there is a mineral earnings boom, the management of potentially disruptive macroeconomic effects requires careful attention.

For other African economies the effects from the development of mineral enclaves have, at best, often been mixed. The Zambian rural economy is still suffering from the negative impact of the copper boom of a generation ago. Nigeria's oil boom was a mixed blessing. In Sierra Leone, easy money from diamonds and gold was an underlying cause of corruption, and there, as in Angola, access to mineral wealth has sustained civil conflict. Even in a country as developed as the Netherlands, the negative effects of the income flows from North-Sea gas gave rise to the concept of 'Dutch disease'. On the other hand, Botswana established a good record of using mineral revenues sensibly, without allowing the access to easy money to distort the economy.

Analysis of future policy options in the event of a mining boom lies beyond the scope of this study. However, there is a period of three to four years before the impact of large increases in mineral exports will be felt. With the experiences of other nations in mind, now is the time to launch a substantial study into the possible impact of a rapid expansion in the mining sector.

Tourism
Tourism is currently growing fast in Tanzania, but further development of the industry requires a more integrated approach than has so far been in evidence. Policies on aircraft landing rights, visa fees and land allocation and their impact on tourist revenues need to be reviewed. There is also a need for greater national participation and an examination of the possible implications of developing tourism in Tanzania.

The foreign exchange earning potential of tourism has still to be seriously exploited. Tanzania has a rich and diverse habitat, with about 247,000 square kilometres, or 25 percent of its total area, set aside as protected areas, including forest reserves, 13 national parks, 22 game reserves and several other conservation areas. Other tourist attractions include Mount Kilimanjaro, an 804 kilometre coastline, Zanzibar, and historical and archaeological sites.

However, despite attractions ranging from game viewing and beach holidays to mountain climbing, game hunting and photographic safaris, the sector's contribution to GDP has fallen far short of its potential. In the past, the Tanzania Tourist Corporation (TTC) and its 13 subsidiary parastatals dominated tourist development. Unfortunately, they failed to take advantage of Tanzania's potential competitive edge. The industry was badly hit by the long period of economic dislocation, and the over-valued exchange rate made Tanzania an unduly expensive destination. Extreme scarcities (of food and drink) also made accommodation rather unattractive.

The replacement of the TTC by the Tanzanian Tourist Board, alongside the introduction of other measures such as the privatisation of hotels, parastatal reform, trade liberalisation, exchange rate adjustment and investment incentives, has substantially changed the environment in which the tourist industry operates. Performance in the sector has improved, although Tanzania is still a relatively expensive destination (as compared, for example, to Kenya).

The number of tourist arrivals increased rapidly during the first three years of the Third Phase Government, from 294,000 arrivals in 1995 to 482,000 arrivals in 1998, and over the same period, estimated tourist earnings increased from Tshs 69,301.70 million to Tshs 114,046.90 million and the sector increased its contribution to GDP from 5.15 percent to 7.57 percent.

Recent growth has largely come from increased occupancy rates rather than expansion of facilities. The number of hotels only increased from 213 in 1997 to 215 in 1998, and the number of rooms from 7,470 to 7,500, but occupancy rates rose from 2,242,500 in 1997 to 2,943,600 in 1998. Earnings per tourist are estimated to have increased from US $878 in 1995 to US $1183 in 1998. However, some actors in the sector have disputed the positive picture suggested by these data and call for further work on the status of the sector.

There are many aspects of policy that deserve further attention. The privatisation of some key assets has been slow. For example, the privatisation of what was once the nation's leading hotel, the Kilimanjaro, has been so slow, that in the transition it has deteriorated sadly. And while Stone Town in Zanzibar has been imaginatively restored, Bagamoyo has been allowed to steadily deteriorate.

Also, aviation policy has tended to be geared to protecting the national carrier, without taking account of the consequences for tourism. Thus, international airlines travel between East African capitals with empty space that they cannot use to carry tourists - if they were allowed to they would have an incentive to promote travel on those routes to Dar es Salaam.

Table 9: Tourism Sector Performance 1990 - 1998 (1992 prices)

Year	Visitors (000's)	Earnings (TShs million)	Earnings Growth (%)	Proportion of GDP (%)
1990	153	20,502.20	-	1.68
1991	187	28,052.55	36.8	2.23
1992	202	40,200.00	43.3	3.15
1993	230	56,134.90	39.6	4.38
1994	262	61,465.90	9.5	4.73
1995	294	69,301.70	12.7	5.15
1996	331	77,862.50	12.4	5.55
1997	359	82,902.50	6.5	5.72
1998	482	114,046.90	37.6	7.57

Source: URT Economic Survey (various years) and ESRF computation

To promote the sector, a draft National Tourism Policy was prepared in 1997. This policy seeks to encourage the development of quality tourism that is culturally and socially responsible, ecologically friendly, environmentally sustainable and economically viable. The policy puts emphasis on increasing the role of the private sector, with the government acting in a catalytic capacity - providing and improving the infrastructure and creating an enabling environment for investment. The draft also has specific tourism policy strategies for product development and marketing, for environmental aspects, for cultural aspects, for international and regional cooperation, for land management and for infrastructural development. There are also strategies for employment and human resource development, community participation, investment incentives, financing, competition and legislation and institutional participation. The list of policy intentions is far reaching, perhaps too ambitious considering the rather limited implementation and budgetary capacity of government. The delineation of the respective roles of the private sector and government makes sense, with the provision of hotels, tour operators and related services being left to the private sector, and the government concentrating on the provision of infrastructure and natural resource management.

Given the potential importance of the contribution of tourism to foreign exchange earnings, support for tourist infrastructure deserves a higher priority in public investment programmes than it has received in the past. However, with scarce resources, the government will need to make clear choices about where it can make an impact. If the promise of the tourist industry is to be realised, a selective and sequenced approach to development will be required, with government marshalling its scarce implementation capacity to pursue achievable targets in given time periods.

Figure 1: Long term performance of non-traditional exports

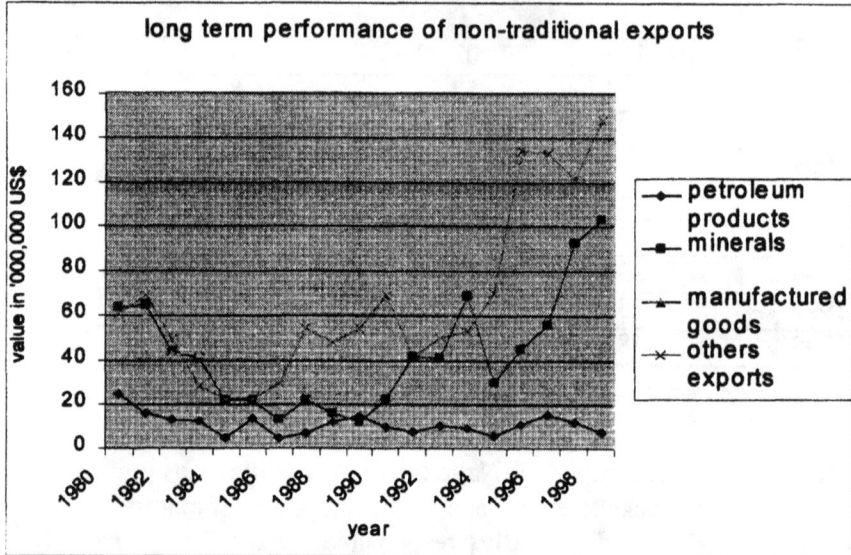

Source: BoT balance of payments department

Industrial export processing

Industrial export processing has been an important component of most of the successes of export led growth of developing economies. To date, this has not developed to any significant extent in Tanzania, partly because of the tardy approach of government towards the creation of effective incentives (e.g. export processing zones). In the current global context, entry into export processing is not easy, given the number of new entrants (e.g. among the follower economies of East Asia, such as Vietnam and Bangladesh). There is also a prospect of heightened competition from established producers (such as Thailand and Indonesia) who severely devalued their currencies in response to the East Asian economic crisis. While there may be fast growth in markets in the future, there is no guarantee that fast growing international markets will lead to success in the industrial export process in Tanzania.[14]

Export prospects over the medium term

After a period in which the response of exports to economic reform was highly encouraging, in 1998, as a result of production and price declines, performance faltered. However, medium term prospects are positive. The growth of mineral and tourist earnings could dramatically change the structure of Tanzanian foreign earnings. The prospects for non-traditional agricultural exports, including cross-border food trade are also good, and the revival of some of the traditional exports should continue. Rapid growth in the export sector coupled with a relaxation in foreign exchange policies, could in the future generate real growth in Tanzania's GDP. Perhaps more importantly, such developments would reduce the excessive dependence of the country and the national budget on foreign aid - a dependence which has been a source of demoralisation, as the spirit of self-reliance has eroded in the past twenty-five years.

Industry and the adjustment process
There are two alternative views of the decade of adjustment in the industrial sector. One robust view is that the period of decline was a necessary stage in reconstruction, clearing away dead wood in preparation for new growth. In this view, many of the earlier investments were inherently non-viable, and efforts to keep some industrial plants in business would have involved a continuing drain on resources. The creation of an efficient industrial sector required the demise of industries that could only survive with levels of protection that would have placed an excessive burden on the rest of the economy.

An alternative view would argue that the surgery was too radical. In this view, there were a number of plants which faced losses because of management problems or infrastructural bottlenecks, but which were potentially viable in the longer term. For example, it might be argued that there is no inherent reason why textile manufacture should not be consistent with Tanzania's long term comparative advantage, and that a more focused effort to sustain some of the capacity which went out of production would have eventually borne fruit.

Whatever the merits of such a debate the industrial sector seems to have turned the corner in the Third Phase period, with growth in the manufacturing sector's contribution to real GDP of 4.8 percent, 5.0 percent and 8.0 percent for 1996, 1997 and 1998. Growth would have been higher if not for infrastructural bottlenecks (including disruptions in power and water supply and in transport). The privatisation of well-established industries producing for the domestic market, such as the breweries and the cigarette company led to the reconstruction of their capital, technology and management and rehabilitation of their plants. Although infrastructural bottlenecks have, in the past, held back production, the resolution of some of the problems which had disrupted electricity and water supplies, have, in the last two years, begun to ease constraints on industrial production.

Box 1: Industrial Growth

A critical weakness of economic policy since Independence has been the failure of efforts to promote industrial production, either of import substitutes for the domestic market, or exports. The performance of the manufacturing sector during the ten years of reforms is summarised in Table 10. The impact of the early stages of economic reform on manufacturing output was largely negative. Increasing competition from imports resulting from trade liberalisation and retrenchment in loss-making parastatals resulted in sharp declines in some sub-sectors. The largest industrial project, the Mufindi Paper Mill, dramatically cut down it's production from a peak of 30,947 mt in 1989 to 7,070 mt in 1998. The textile industry, both public and private, was particularly badly hit by competition from imports. A number of industrial projects from the 1970s never produced any significant output (e.g. the notorious Morogoro shoe factory; some cashew processing factories and textile mills). Unfortunately, the only lasting impact of such investments has been on the nation's debt burden. Even some smaller firms that had done well through preferential access to import support under the pre-reform foreign exchange regime were unable to compete in a more competitive environment.

Some lessons of failed industrialisation:

The industrialisation effort faltered for many reasons. Location was haphazard, with too little coordination with infrastructural investment. Following the severe deterioration in the foreign exchange situation after 1978 new industrial capacity could not be utilised because of the lack of foreign currency to provide inputs.

Probably the most critical mistake at the microeconomic level was the failure to provide adequately for the management requirements of the new industries which were being developed, so that even with the comfort of highly protected domestic markets, they failed to produce and find markets. Many large, fairly sophisticated investments were put in place without plausible arrangements for management and technical support. Where managers and professionals were trained, they were often given responsibilities before they had sufficient experience working in cooperation with more seasoned staff.

Looking back on the 1970s, many things went wrong with the industrialisation effort. Microeconomic factors, such as poor project design and inadequate attention to management requirements took their toll. Sectoral imbalances meant that many projects were frustrated by infrastructural bottlenecks. Macroeconomic disequilibrium affected all economic activity, including industry. It is difficult to establish any one clear lesson for failure.

How far the poor export performance that contributed to the foreign exchange crisis was the result of the industrialisation effort is unclear. At first sight, it might appear that the Basic Industrialisation Strategy was seeking to promote industrial growth at the expense of agriculture. However, agricultural disincentives did not result from the classic mechanism of surplus transfers to finance industry - monopolistic single channel marketing transferred surpluses to a bureaucratic "black hole" of inefficiency, rather than to investment activities. Also, a large part of the industrial investment resulted in idle capacity rather than output, so agriculturists did not have to subsidise industry by buying expensive import substitutes. Nevertheless, the industrial investment programme was part of the ambitious capital formation effort of the 1970s which gave rise to the macroeconomic disequilibrium, which in turn placed a heavy burden on the agricultural export sector.

Although the main thrust of the industrialisation effort was to produce import substitutes for the East African market, some explicit efforts were made to produce industrial exports. These efforts included the ill-fated World Bank financed Morogoro shoe factory, which deserves its place in the history of Tanzanian development failures alongside the groundnut scheme. There were somewhat more plausible Swedish supported efforts to promote small industry export manufacture, in cooperation with Swedish firms, and investments in sisal and cashewnut processing. Efforts to generate industrial exports met with little success, while traditional agricultural exports declined, so that the overall result was that exports declined as a ratio to GDP, while dependence on imports for industrial products and fuel persisted - the resulting gap being filled by aid.

Table 10: Performance of the Manufacturing Sector in Tanzania 1987-1998 (1992 prices, %)

Year	Manuf. GDP Growth	Share in Total Growth	Manuf. Export Growth	Share in Total Exports	Share in NT Exports	Average Capacity Utiliz.
1987		8.9				
1988	3.1	8.7				
1989	5.2	9.0				
1990	4.1	8.8				
1991	1.9	8.7		19.4	43.7	50
1992	-4.1	8.2	-8.7	16.0	38.8	38
1993	0.6	8.2	-19.0	11.8	28.4	50
1994	0.2	8.1	48.0	14.8	42.2	46
1995	1.6	7.9	41.9	16.0	36.5	-
1996	4.8	8.0	1.4	14.6	35.3	48
1997	5.0	8.1	-5.7	14.5	29.2	-
1998	8.0	8.4	-31.0	10.7	21.8	55

Source: URT Economic Survey (various) and BoT (1999)

However, while the signs of revival in industrial production are welcome, in certain crucial respects industrial performance is still limited. The large scale industries which are doing well are mainly those producing for the local market, which enjoy high levels of natural protection (e.g. brewing and cement), and which developed in East Africa at the earliest stages of industrialisation. There has been no breakthrough in manufacturing production for export. In fact, manufacturing exports declined over the 1995-98 period.[15]

Fast growth in industrial exports has made a significant, and, in many cases, the major contribution to the performance of those countries that have achieved successful transformation over the past generation (not only in the East Asian tigers, but also closer to home in Mauritius). A challenge facing the Third Phase Government is the creation of those conditions that favour the growth of manufacturing exports; that is, a dynamic and competitive industrial structure.

Future industrial policy
Taking a long view, if Tanzania is to develop it must experience a technological revolution in industrial production and organisation and eventually move into high technology manufacturing. In the twenty-first century, success in industry will be based on new technologies, new

management and organisational techniques, linkages and networks.

Tanzania faces fundamental constraints on industrial development relating to institutional weakness, inadequate infrastructure and a low level of human resource development. There are few Tanzanians with the experience and access to capital needed to become large scale industrial entrepreneurs. The civil service and the professions have no experience in servicing a successful industrial sector. Therefore, the accent will need to shift towards learning and building of capabilities for attaining competitiveness in domestic markets and in exports to the region and to global markets.

Experience in the reform period demonstrates that even if opening up the economy to competition from imports is a necessary condition for developing a dynamic and competitive industrial sector, it is in itself far from sufficient. In principle a case can be made for Government intervention, focusing on supportive policies to help enterprises upgrade their technologies and competitiveness. It can be argued that Government intervention is needed to build an institutional infrastructure (e.g. development finance facilities), provide technical training, develop quality standards, disseminate market information, develop applied research in appropriate fields for industrial development and, in general, promote investments and technology flows.

In practice, difficulty arises because the Government lacks the capacity to design and implement selective interventions, and to respond to international developments in markets and modern technology. To pursue an interventionist industrial policy the government will have to start with an active capacity building initiative in industrial policy management and administration, to develop understanding among the Tanzanian civil service professionals and political leadership, of the requirements for success. In the first instance, this will require the study of successful market orientated industrial development efforts elsewhere in the world.

One aspect of industrial policy that requires some thought relates to the actors who are likely to be leading industrialists. Acceleration in industrial growth and promotion of industrial exports will require a high degree of cooperation between potential industrial investors and government. This will require more effective two-way communication between industrialists and government. For example, existing industrialists still display a preference for investments to supply the domestic market. To shift their attention to the important task of developing industrial exports a systematic dialogue may be required between the government leadership and the investing community. However, in the liberalised, privatised economy, in the medium term, large scale investors in industry will be mainly foreign investors or members of minority communities in Tanzania. It may be necessary to develop a mechanism for the formal exchange of views between key industrialists and State House.[16] In this context, efforts towards the formation of the Tanzania Private Sector Foundation and the Tanzania National Business Council are encouraging institutional development in the right direction.

Capital formation

A third constraint on output is the size of the capital stock. Over the longer term, higher growth in GDP will require higher rates of capital formation, to expand the capacity to produce. Early Tanzanian plans tended to concentrate on capital as the constraint on growth, and a good deal of attention was given to raising the investment rate. However, experience has demonstrated that while higher investment rates are a necessary condition for increased growth, they are not in themselves sufficient.

In the 1970s, large investments were put into projects that failed to generate the expected output, and success in raising the rate of investment was not matched by commensurate output growth. Thus the efficient allocation of investment funds is even more important than the level of capital formation. Nevertheless, most examples of accelerated growth in the world's economies have been associated with high rates of capital formation.

The available data suggests that during the period of the Third Phase Government there has been a decline in investment. In the period 1990-92, the ratio of gross fixed capital formation to GDP was 26/27 percent, by 1996-97 that ratio had fallen to 16 percent, with some recovery in 1998. The fact that the fall in investment did not lead to falls in output could be an indication that the efficiency of investment increased. It should be noted that the type of investment which declined most drastically - parastatal investment - had been associated with negative incremental capital output ratios in the 1970s and 1980s.

The falling investment effort reflects the decline in public sector (government and parastatal) investment, from 9 percent of GDP in 1990-92 to 3-4 percent of GDP in 1996-97. This decline was mainly accounted for by a sharp reduction in parastatal investment, reflecting the de-emphasis on the role of the state sector. The decline in public investment was offset by an increase in private investment in the early 1990s, but from 1994 there was a decline in the percentage of GDP allocated to private investment.[17] Although this decline was reversed in 1998, private investment is still below levels required for the private sector to play the role expected of it in the reformed economy.

Table 11: Capital formation 1995-1998 (1992 prices)

Year	1995	1996	1997	1998
Buildings:				
Residential	25999	28563	20722	22533
Rural own-account	46581	49259	43465	46990
Non-residential	26753	28791	25703	20653
TOTAL	**99333**	**104392**	**91422**	**90176**
Other Works:				
Land improvements	5719	7388	9638	1479
Roads and bridges	6291	3079	2575	19708
Water Supply	962	471	1318	10674
Others	11959	15670	15281	7308
TOTAL	**24931**	**26608**	**28812**	**39169**
Equipment:				
Transport equipment	55443	51868	47549	53182
Other equipment	102088	85552	91907	114693
TOTAL	**157531**	**137420**	**139456**	**167875**
Total fixed capital formation	281795	268420	259690	297220
Increase in stocks	3764	3794	3825	3855
Capital formation	*285559*	*272214*	*263515*	*301075*

Source: *URT Economic Survey 1998*

Table 12: Capital formation by public and private sectors (at current prices in Tshs million)

Sector	1985	1987	1989	1991	1993	1995	1996	1997	1998
Central Govt.	2202	4826	5384	16151	52170	23727	20087	25860	128079
Parastatals	4428	20489	61817	78775	74773	75618	111555	108245	28088
Institutions	152	275	355	926	2322	2635	3371	3533	29148
Total Public Sector	6782	25590	67556	95852	129265	101980	135013	137638	185315
Private Sector	12942	45469	44651	186576	300280	489915	498902	554762	641778
Total Fixed Capital	19724	71059	112207	282428	429545	591895	633915	692400	827093
Increase in Stocks	587	1700	2356	3645	4002	5856	6640	8403	9914
Total Capital Formation	20311	72759	114563	286073	433547	597751	640555	700803	837007

Source: *URT Economic Survey 1998*

It should also be recognised that some public sector investment programmes are crucial to the performance of the economy, and far from competing with private investment they form a necessary prerequisite to higher levels of private investment. In recent years the most notable example of such investment has been the government/donor effort to rehabilitate the road system.

The first Integrated Road Programme (IRP-1) focused on restoring the main trunk road system to a reasonable operating level. The IRP-2 aimed to mobilise small scale private sector firms in rural roads construction. About 60,000 kilometres of rural roads were supposed to be implemented by small labour-based contractors. However, in practice only 4,500 kilometres of the rural road network were estimated to have been rehabilitated by the programme by 1998 and out of these only 1300 kilometres have been identified on the basis of agricultural need. This inadequate performance was due to the fact that district councils still had too little capacity to carry out the role allotted to them. In 1997, the IRP-2 activities were halted for the purpose of restructuring the project.

The Road Fund which begun in 1998/99 is intended to contribute to improvement of the effectiveness of the management of the roads network and finance maintenance, but the available funds are inadequate for the task. More financial and personnel resources will be required to support the autonomous road agency (TANROADS) which was established in 1998/99 and which is expected to become operational in 1999/2000.

The achievement of sustained high rates of capital formation is more likely if domestic savings are available to fund a significant proportion of investment. The GDP data suggest that in the mid-1990s there was little domestic savings (in 1994/95 the domestic savings ratio was estimated to be negative, at -0.2 percent of GDP). Recent performance indicates some improvement in that regard, with the domestic savings ratio estimated to have risen to 7 percent by 1997/98. This is largely explained by tight budget policy, which reduced public consumption and government spending.

Human and institutional development

Economists have always been aware that economic growth is not completely, or even primarily, explained by such readily measurable factors as capital formation or foreign exchange. Econometric models developed in the 1950s and 1960s which attempted to attribute growth to capital and labour left a significant residual unexplained, which was identified as the contribution of technical progress to growth. In the early literature on economic development and history, there was a rich discussion of the impact of social, cultural and religious factors on economic performance.

It is evident that the relative performance of countries cannot be simply explained by access to physical resources. Studies of the effectiveness of foreign aid have indicated that there is a big variation in the productive impact of aid, depending on the policy environment, which is in turn dependent on political and social processes. In recent years there have been new contributions to the understanding of the role of institutions in influencing economic performance, which has contributed to a deeper understanding of the institutional prerequisites for the effective operations of markets and business organisations.[18] Much of the discussion of the role of social and institutional factors in development is speculative and sometimes not immediately relevant to policy. However, a number of concrete and practical suggestions are made in this literature. In relation to Tanzanian development, there are a series of inter-locking issues, which should be given priority in the medium term policy agenda. In this volume discussion focuses on four areas:

(a) *The capacity of government institutions*. The ability of government to set public sector resource allocation priorities, deliver services and fashion an appropriate institutional environment for economic activity is crucial for development. Over recent decades, variations in such capacity has been an important contributory factor to the difference in performance between the economies of Africa, characterised by weak and decaying government capacity, and the relatively effective states of East Asia.[19]

(b) *Investment in human capital*. A related set of issues concerns the development of human knowledge and skills. This is, in part, a matter of formal education, but also relates to on-the-job training and "learning by doing" (or "unlearning by not doing" - the loss of knowledge and skills resulting from failure to use them, either because of lack of job opportunities or a negative work environment).

(c) *The institutional environment conditioning business activity*. The legal, administrative and incentive structures which provide the environment within which the various actors in the economy operate (sometimes summarised as the "enabling environment") are crucial factors in development. A legal and administrative system that is fair, predictable in its impact, and transparent in operation, is an important asset. For example, uncertainty about land tenure as a result of inadequate laws and lax land administration is a disincentive to investment in property development. A capricious and corrupt application of government regulations increases the uncertainty and therefore the cost of transactions.

(d) *Social capital*. A recent addition to the discussion of development has been the consideration of the importance of social capital. For the purposes of this discussion that can be taken to mean the network of formal and informal organisations and relationships on which individuals can draw for support and stimulus, and which promote joint efforts in the pursuit of social and economic goals. A full discussion of this range of issues is beyond the scope of this short study, but it is important to flag the point. Households survive and prosper not only on the basis of formal employment and income and from services provided by the state, but also from their connections with the extended family, church and mosque, local community, academic and sports organisations, to mention a few. For the migrant from rural areas, survival and entry into the urban economy may depend on access to informal networks of family and community.[20]

The challenge of universal provision

One of the greatest challenges faced by the Third Phase Government has been the improvement of social service delivery. From the point of view of the public, reasonable access to social services such as health, education and water supply are critical components of family welfare. It is not surprising, therefore, that in its 1995 election manifesto CCM set for itself the task of consolidating, developing and improving social service delivery, especially in the sectors of education, health, water and housing.

Investment in human capital has come to be recognised as a critical requirement for economic performance. From a political point of view social service delivery is also of critical importance, as it represents a pervasive point of contact between the citizen and the state. The deterioration of the social services, along with the poor state of economic infrastructure has acted to erode public confidence in the government and contributed to widespread cynicism.

The issues the Third Phase Government has had to address need to be placed in the historical context of the national effort to extend social services to the mass population in the 1970s and the crisis confronting the system by the early 1980s. Tanzania came to Independence with an extremely weak social infrastructure, even in comparison to other African colonies. In 1961, the health system consisted of a few hospitals and private doctors in urban areas, religious mission services and traditional healers in rural areas. The education system was stratified by racial categories and most households obtained water from natural sources.

The Arusha Declaration promulgated in 1967, and its subsequent elaboration of social goals in the second five-year plan and sectoral documents (such as the considerable literature on 'Education for Self Reliance') articulated an egalitarian vision of social service provision. Strategies were devised to utilise scarce resources and extend basic education, health, and urban housing and, later, water facilities to the mass of the population. In relation to education, this was also taken to imply changes in the content of education to make it more relevant to the needs of the predominantly rural population.

In setting these objectives, Tanzania in essence adopted a 'basic-needs' approach almost a decade before that term became fashionable among the donor community. The government's basic approach was to provide both basic and complex social services to the whole population, using uniform population based standards for construction and staffing. These services were to be provided at no charge to the users, but financed through tax revenue and donor support.

The importance of the commitment to universal provision should be understood in the context of the re-emergence of poverty alleviation as the main focus of concern within the donor community. The poor only gain access to services when they are universally available. If, for example, only 70 percent of children are in primary school, those 30 percent not receiving schooling will tend to come from poorer families. The reasons for failure to achieve the Arusha social objectives pursued in the 1970s therefore deserve some attention.

During the early seventies, the goals of mass provision were pursued with some vigour. In the case of education, for example, even the ambitious goals for expanding primary education set out in the Second Plan were seen to be too timid, and in 1974 the decision was made to push for universal primary education and universal literacy over the short-term. Similar strategies were adopted in the health and water sectors, where rapid steps were taken to ensure universal provision. As the objective was to provide universal coverage on an egalitarian basis, services were in general supplied to the consumer without charge at the point of delivery.

The historical record

Education

The World Bank Report on Tanganyika (1960) just prior to Independence summarised the situation. Education was divided into primary school, middle school and secondary school, comprising four standards, each ranging from standard I to standard XII. The majority of middle and secondary schools were boarding schools, making this level of education costly. 45 percent of school-age children entered standard I but only 75 percent of those enrolled reached standard IV. In 1960, less than 1 in 8 of those enrolled in standard I reached standard XII. Girls made up only 38 percent of those enrolled at standard I with the disparity growing to only 7 percent of those enrolled at standard XII. There was no university college in Tanganyika.

In the early years following Independence, the main thrust of educational policy was geared to training Tanzanians to replace expatriates in managerial, technical and professional roles. The long term perspective in the first Five Year Plan (1964-1969) was to achieve substantial self-sufficiency in that regard by 1980. Given the scarcity of resources, it was intended to do this by setting the targets for the output of the secondary and tertiary levels of education in order to meet the demand projected by manpower planners. Although this implied some restraint, the growth rates set for secondary and tertiary education were still quite high, because of the low initial base.

Significant growth in primary enrolment was also targeted, but given the limited existing coverage the achievement of universal coverage was set far in the future. In fact, when the second five-year plan (1969-1974) was being formulated, calculations indicated that at the existing rate of expansion, universal primary school provision would not be achieved until the middle of the next century.

In the education sector, the Government was the primary provider of services from primary through to tertiary institutions. During the period of high mobilisation, particularly in the 1970s, the number of primary schools and teachers increased as a result of campaign style programmes. The government sought to make primary education universal, compulsory and affordable to the poorest households. Thus, it oriented the curriculum to rural life while limiting secondary school and university intake. The government also tried to increase the equity of admissions into secondary schools through a quota system that gave preferential treatment to disadvantaged groups.

Expansion in primary education was rapid, with increases in the number of pupils in primary schools and the number of education sector workers. The majority of the 10,900 primary schools now in operation were constructed during the 1970s, when the aim was for each village to have its own primary school. Most of the 40 teacher training colleges now in operation were also opened during that period.

Secondary school enrolment expanded at a much slower pace. This was due to deliberate rationing of secondary schooling as part of government efforts to provide universal literacy and coordinate outputs from the educational system with the nation's manpower requirements. Between 1971 and 1981, enrolments in secondary schools (nearly all of which were operated by the government), grew by only about 24,000 students, and the enrolment rate has remained static at about 4 percent (World Bank, 1995).

Health
In the health sector, the number of government operated rural health centres more than tripled between 1969 and 1978 and the number of dispensaries nearly doubled. There were only 50 health centres and 1,444 dispensaries in 1969, by 1978/97 these had risen to 183 and 2,282 respectively (World Bank, 1995). Most of the 107 institutions now training health personnel were opened during that decade and large numbers of rural medical aides, medical assistants, medical officers and nurses were trained and deployed to the rural areas. As a result, the number of doctors increased more than three-fold and the number of medical assistants, rural medical aides and health assistants increased by a factor of 10. This expansion allowed about 90 percent of the population to be within 10 kilometres of a health facility and nearly three-quarters to be within 5 kilometres of public health services.

Health services were directed toward the rural areas and basic health needs. This included family planning services which were integrated with maternal and child health. At the base of the referral pyramid and close to the village, there were rural dispensaries and health centres, while at the apex there were consultant hospitals in large cities.

Water

In the water sector, the government instituted a policy of free water supplies for rural areas. The Government's goal was to provide the rural population with potable water supplies within 400 metres of most households. The Government budget financed all water supply investments, with substantial material and technical assistance from donor agencies. The construction of water systems were based on Regional Water Master Plans (RWMP), which typically projected water system construction and the optimal domestic and agricultural use of all water resources over a 20 year time frame. Under RWMPs, donor financed blueprints for improved water schemes were created in nearly all regions, and large scale construction was initiated. Between 1971 and 1980, the proportion of the population with access to improved water supplies nationally increased from 12 to 47 percent.

As momentum in the water sector picked up, similar centrally planned activities were initiated to expand access to sanitation facilities. In 1973, the government introduced the latrinisation campaign, "Mtu in Iffy". This campaign, which required that each household should have and use a latrine, was given additional emphasis after the cholera outbreak in 1977. As a result, latrine coverage in rural areas was estimated to have increased from 20 percent to 50 percent between 1973 and 1980.

Reflections on the experience

This early success did not last and in the 1980s economic crisis severely impeded the government's efforts to provide universal basic social services. As the population's expectations for services increased the government's capacity to deliver them dramatically declined.

Twenty years on it remains important to understand the causes of earlier failure. The goals articulated in the Arusha Declaration and in subsequent policies were worthy and incorporated a vision which remains relevant. Lessons to be learnt from the earlier failure may be important for renewed efforts to expand the coverage of public services. Many of the characteristics and problems of the current system reflect the impact of earlier policies.

At one level, the weaknesses in social service provision that the Third Phase Government has had to tackle can be explained by the weak performance of the economy. The extended fiscal difficulties (from the late

1970s onwards) resulted in the savage reduction in the real wages of government staff, with the survival strategies of government employees affecting their performance (e.g. the pursuit of extra income sources). The declining real resource allocations to the social services also resulted in severe shortages in the supporting inputs required for staff to perform their duties. To some degree therefore, the decline in social service provision was just a part of the larger economic malaise.

However, it could also be argued that the economic difficulties facing the country brought into sharper focus weaknesses that were inherent in the strategies adopted. The rush to expand services took insufficient account of the institutional and human requirements to maintain the services provided.[21] While problems were exacerbated by severe fiscal constraints, the origins of the systemic difficulties were not solely financial. The lack of appropriate skills to maintain systems and the weak institutional arrangements to ensure effective operations and maintenance were systemic problems in all public expansion programmes. The recurrent cost burden following large capital investments in education, health and water services and the recruitment of large numbers of personnel was enormous. While donors had been willing and able to finance much of the capital cost, financing the recurrent cost was largely left to the government.

Managing the network of schools, health facilities and water systems was made difficult by the limited transportation to rural areas. The problems were made worse by lack of coordination and changing lines of responsibility and authority. Local government, which had been abolished in 1973, was reinstituted in 1983. Education and health sector employees, technically accountable to central ministries and supervised by regional authorities, were employed by the local governments, which had neither adequate financing nor management capacity. Donor efforts were sometimes poorly coordinated with core supervisory and service delivery functions in the health sector. External assistance to the water sector was poorly integrated into the government's existing structure and little indigenous capacity was built to maintain the systems after the termination of consultant contracts.

At the early stages of structural adjustment, too little attention was given to understanding how to improve the effectiveness of delivery of those economic and social services which remained the responsibility of the state. Fiscal constraints took their toll, resulting in further sharp declines in the real wages of public employees and chronic inadequacy of input supply.

However, in the social sectors, as in economic activities, a spontaneous process of adjustment began, ahead of changes in policy, as consumers with the means found their own ways of ensuring access. This process was sometimes chaotic, as it involved (typically illegal) private payments for priority access to services that were supposedly free, and led to the spread of moonlighting by professional staff.

The problem of weak morale and lack of commitment among some officials responsible for service delivery can be seen as part of a larger picture of weak civil service performance. However, proposed civil service reforms, which involve moving towards a leaner and well-paid civil service, are not a viable strategy for universal service provision as they do not address the problems of a highly labour intensive service delivery system. Inevitably, the broad provision of social and other critical government services, such as law and order, demands the employment of large numbers, determined by the size of the population and necessary staffing ratios (class size; rural dispensary staffing and coverage). The large numbers required for the mass provision of such services places limits on the degree to which the number of public employees can be reduced. For example, reducing the proportion of the population in public service to the levels of the 'efficient'colonial days would also imply a return to colonial levels of service provision.

In turn, the size of public employment determines the possible real salary level. In general, recurrent staffing costs must be met from government revenues, which are in turn limited by the average income level and the attainable levels of taxation, consistent with economic growth. This suggests that underlying the crisis in service provision is a real and unresolved dilemma. There may be a choice, which is unavoidable, between the highly selective provision of services by well-paid staff and more widespread provision at low unit costs (and therefore low staff incentives).

Faced with this underlying dilemma, from the early 1990s the government has sought to re-define its core functions in relation to social service delivery. In this process, it is increasingly accepted that non-governmental partners should share the burden of developing the social sectors.

The status of social service delivery

Provision of social services is still dominated by the public sector, especially at the primary and tertiary levels where more than 80 percent of both education and health facilities are owned by the state. Even after the first decade of structural adjustment, private expenditures on social services remained very modest.

In terms of household spending, for the average household in 1993, about 72 percent, was for food, while health accounted for only 1.9 percent and education only 1.4 percent. Urban residents and the rich spent more on health in both absolute and percentage terms than did the rural poor.

Education accounted for only 1.2 percent of expenditures in both rural areas and Dar es Salaam, but 2.0 percent in other cities.

Status of the education sector

The education sector is divided into five tiers: pre-primary, primary, secondary, teacher, and tertiary/higher education.

At the pre-school level, hardly 10 percent of the population have access, although in principle some facilities have been formalised and integrated in the formal school system. Non-government and government pre-schools constitute 68 percent and 32 percent respectively (Mukyanuzi et al 1998:2). There are 11,290 primary schools (1998 data), out of which 99.8 percent are government and only 0.2 percent are non-government. Around 4 million pupils are enrolled in government primary schools. By 1998, Net Enrolment Ratio (NER) and Gross Enrolment Ratio (GER) were 55 percent and 77.9 percent respectively, with a teacher pupil ratio of 1:35. Repetition, especially in lower classes, is high (19 percent), while the drop out rate is 6 percent. At the primary level the gender balance is even. Teaching is mainly organised in a single session and schools are co-educational. The physical facilities vary enormously, but many buildings are in poor shape, with furnishings and supplies of teaching materials woefully inadequate.

In principle, primary school teachers are expected to have had a secondary education background plus two years of professional training. However, only about 40 percent receive such preparation, while the rest have a primary education background.

Average expenditure on education as a percentage of GDP is approximately 3.0 percent, while public expenditure on education as a percentage of government expenditure averages 24.4 percent. Out of this, 68 percent is allocated to the primary level. The relative emphasis on the primary sector is in line with the conventional development thinking of the last two decades (e.g. of the World Bank) that the highest returns to investments in education are reaped at the primary level.

However, Tanzanian experience also demonstrates that there is a necessary link between primary and secondary education. If it is accepted that primary school teachers should have received a secondary school education, staffing of primary schools at the requisite level requires a parallel effort to expand secondary education. Moreover, in a free labour market, this may require over-supply of secondary school leavers, as the incentives affordable at the primary level are unlikely to make primary teaching a first career choice in a tight labour market.

The structure of secondary education also reflects long term policy decisions. The decision made as early as the mid-1960s to restrain secondary and higher education to levels required to supply the needs identified in manpower plans meant that the number of places offered in public secondary schools was much lower than in neighbouring countries. It was at this level that unsatisfied demand for education appeared. However, in an effort to establish a fair distribution of access (across regions and religions) to this scarce and critical facility, most secondary education was brought within the public sector with, for example, the old church run schools being transferred to the state sector. When these changes were instituted more than thirty years ago, the only exceptions were the religious seminaries and international schools serving the expatriate community. However, as an aspiring middle class developed, the scarcity of places in government schools meant that parents had to seek other solutions. For the very well off, that meant seeking education abroad (the location depending on the size of the wallet).

In the 1990s there was a decisive shift in policy. Government accepted that the non-government sector had a more important role to play in secondary education. At the very least, it made little sense to force those seeking alternatives to government schooling to use foreign exchange to purchase education abroad.

By 1998 private secondary schools constituted 47 percent (369 schools) with an enrolment of 109 thousand students taught by 5075 teachers (a teacher student ratio of 1:21.5). There were 416 government secondary schools with enrolment of 116,556 students taught by 6359 teachers (i.e. a teacher student ratio of 1:18). Entry into government secondary schools is based on a competitive primary education examination. The national selection rate is 7 percent.

Repetition and dropout rates in government secondary schools are undocumented but they are estimated at less than 5 percent (in private secondary schools, the drop out rate is well over 10 percent). Out of the sectoral budget, 8.7 percent is allocated to this sub-sector. In most schools, teaching is organised on a single session and over 60 percent of the schools are co-educational. About 19 percent of the teachers are degree holders while the rest hold diplomas.

Within the private sector, a bi-modal distribution is emerging. Most private schools have less qualified teachers than the government schools with about 5 percent degree holders, 55 percent diploma holders and 40 percent with qualifications below a diploma. However, the seminaries and a small minority of elite schools have staff with qualifications that match or exceed those of the government schools.[22]

Teacher education in 1998 had an enrolment of 9,136 and 316 students in public and private colleges respectively. The number of tutors was 1,004 and 58 in public and private colleges respectively (staff student rations of 1:9.1 and 1:5.5). Entry into public teachers' colleges depends upon success in the Form IV Examination, Division III being the lowest qualification. The sub-sector gets 2.3 percent of the sectoral budget. Repetition is only permissible under exceptional cases.

Technical education is not provided privately. There are three public institutions with a total student population of 1,797 taught by 257 tutors (a staff student ratio of 1:7). Out of the 257 tutors, 23.4 percent had postgraduate qualifications, 25.6 percent a bachelor's degree and 51 percent a diploma. Entry is highly competitive, with most entrants scoring Division I or II with a strong maths and natural science background. The sub-sector gets about 1.6 percent of the sectoral budget.[23]

At the higher education level, enrolment in public university colleges is 10,653 with 1,141 lecturers (i.e. a staff student ratio of 1:9) (1998 data). Financial resources allocated constitute 19 percent of the education sector budget. Although universities are allocated almost one-fifth of the education budget to the universities (more than twice the allocation to government secondary education, with less than one-tenth the number of students), the perception in the universities is that they suffer from chronic under funding. The small number of places means that entry is highly competitive, based on both entrance and/or national examinations. Despite this, the drop out rate is quite high (30-40 percent), especially in medical and natural science related specialisations. In Tanzania four private university colleges have an enrolment of 516 (Mukyanuzi et al, 1999).

Status of the health sector

The Tanzania health care system consists of 164 hospitals, 269 health centres and 3,078 dispensaries in 1998. 36 percent of the hospitals, 78 percent of the health centres and 66 percent of the dispensaries are public facilities. The rest are owned by charitable organisations, NGOs and private for profit care providers. It is estimated that 93 percent of the population live within 10kms from a health facility and about 72 percent within 5kms (MoH, 1998).

The allocation of resources is highly skewed towards tertiary hospital services and at each level a disproportionate share of resources are spent on personal emoluments. In spite of government emphasis on preventive care in policy documents for the past three decades, analysis of recent government expenditure figures indicate that about 77 percent of government resources are spent on curative services. Allocation of personnel tends to favour urban areas (MoH, 1996).

The post-Arusha policies for the health services emphasised public and charitable health provision, and discouraged private practice. This policy was relaxed in 1983. In recent years there has been a fast growth of the private sector. While this has resulted in an expanded and more flexible health service, it has also increased an existing bias towards serving the urban areas. For example, in 1993, there were 500 newly registered care providers, 253 (50.1 percent) of whom were in Dar es Salaam (ibid). This is not surprising, as private provision responds to income expenditure location.

Key health indicators remain depressing. The Infant Mortality Rate (IMR) is 92, compared to 66 for Kenya. The under-5 Mortality Rate is 141 and the Maternal Mortality Rate (MMR) is estimated at 200–400 per 100,000 births. Adult mortality rates are twice as high as those in Britain. For young adults aged 15-34 years, the mortality rates in Tanzania are 8-10 times those in Britain, (ESRF 1998:30). Although some of the leading traditional sources of morbidity and death have decreased, the rapid expansion in AIDS is reversing earlier improvements in mortality rates.

The prevalence of preventable diseases places a large burden on the curative health system. Malaria constitutes the most common reason for attendance at outpatient clinics and hospitals admissions. Respiratory infections, including pneumonia, also consume a large proportion of curative resources. Diarrhoea diseases also account for a large share of outpatient visits. On nutrition: 29 percent of the children under five years of age are moderately malnourished and 47 percent are stunted. Malnutrition rates are low in the first year of life when babies are predominantly breast fed, but increase sharply in the second year of life. Malnutrition is most severe in rural areas and least severe in Dar es Salaam.[24]

In addition to stunting, low birth-weight suggested that maternal malnutrition is a significant problem. The Demographic and Health Survey of 1991/92 estimated the incidence of low birth-weights in Tanzania to be 18 percent. The high incidence of low birth-weights results from many factors, such as poor nutritional status of women, poor health care and a high rate of malaria and other infections during pregnancy. Nutritional status of children is closely related to mother's education, an effect to be seen even at relatively low levels of education. Nearly half of all children under-fives born to mothers with no education showed signs of moderate stunting, while only about a quarter of children born to mothers with post-primary education were stunted.

The major nutritional problems are protein energy malnutrition, nutritional anaemia, iodine deficiency disorders and vitamin A deficiency. The main causes of these problems include inadequate food intake resulting from low feeding frequency with insufficient energy and key nutrients. The majority of the victims are pregnant women and children below the age of five. Data on the prevalence of protein energy malnutrition indicate that five percent of under-fives are severely affected and about 47 percent are moderately affected. This condition also affects 3 percent of pregnant women severely and around 10 percent moderately. Nutritional anaemia is estimated to affect 45 percent of under-fives and as many as 80 percent of pregnant women. An estimated 25 percent of the population (5.6 million people) are affected by iodine deficiency and an estimated 1.3 million people suffer from vitamin A deficiency. There is general ignorance about such nutritional problems at the policy making, technical and community level. Although many of the solutions are within the resource capacity of households and communities, effective initiatives to combat malnutrition have yet to be demonstrated.

Official estimates suggest that the population is still growing at a rate that will double the total population over the next 25 years. However, the growth rate is likely to come down through the impact of the AIDS pandemic - but in a very unsatisfactory way, as the impact will be mostly on the working-age population, resulting in a rise in dependency ratios.

A high fertility rate poses problems for women, households and at the national level. Current use of contraceptives stands at 7 percent. The majority of these (52 percent) use the pill and 25 percent prefer sterilisation, the remaining 23 percent use injectables and condoms.

Status of the water sector

Official estimates in 1998 indicated a rural and urban coverage level of 49 percent and 81 percent respectively. These rates are based on installed capacity. Effective coverage is actually much lower than in 1992, for example, 30 percent of the 10,961 rural schemes were not operating at all. An unspecified number were operating below capacity due to a range of reasons, including inadequate supply of recurrent inputs.[25]

A range of technologies are used in the provision of water, including gravity piped, pressure pumped, deep and shallow wells, open wells and dams. The range of technologies in itself is a problem as it makes procurement of spare parts, maintenance and containment cost difficult.

During the 1980s, government expenditure on water and sanitation declined. For example, in the 1980/81 budget, the government devoted about US $51.5 million to the sector but by 1989/90, government expenditures on water had declined to US $9.2 million. Donor interest in large scale investment dropped off dramatically.[26]

The majority of Tanzanian households pay for water with their labour. In rural areas, an average household spends about three hours a day collecting water - over 1,000 hours per year. Even in urban areas, households on average spend about 1.5 hours a day collecting water from outside the home.

Policy

Stated Policy
The problems faced in the social sector have stimulated re-thinking about the roles of the government and other actors in service provision. The government has sought increasingly to focus on the delivery of basic health and education services, while liberalising private sector participation. The intention is to define the public sector's core functions and concentrate the bulk of public funds in them.

Documents articulating shifting approaches include the 1994 Social Sector Strategy (SSS) and the 1995 Social Sector Review (SSR). The 1995 CCM election manifesto and the 1995 presidential speech both emphasised social services expansion and quality improvement.

Characteristics of the new policy focus include:

(a) concentrating scarce public funds on core activities of government;
(b) striking a more productive balance between personnel and other inputs within the social sectors;
(c) decentralising authority to the local level;
(d) relaxing constraints on private sector participation in provision of social services;
(e) promoting improved standards; and
(d) shifting control over resource allocation closer to the household and promoting household investment in human capital.

Performance

Performance of the education sector
Government has sought to allocate more resources to the basic social sectors, as reflected in the guidelines for the preparation of the sixth rolling plan and forward budget for the period 1998/99-2000/01. 24 percent of the budget was to go to social sectors compared to 11 percent in 1995/96, 14.3 percent in 1996/97 and 15.5 percent in 1997/98. Out of these social sector allocations, 60-65 percent was allocated to basic social services (basic education, primary health care and rural water supply) compared to 55-57 percent allocated to basic social services before 1995. However, intra-sectoral allocation to higher education increased from 9.4 percent to 17.6 percent between 1995 and 1998. Percentage allocations to secondary education have been reduced from 8.1 to 7.4 percent and have remained constant for technical education (Mukyanuzi, 1999).

User charges have increased. At the basic education level contributions for primary education have risen from Tshs 1,000 to Tshs 2,000, secondary school fees have risen from Tshs 30,000 to Tshs 40,000 for day schools and boarding school fees have risen from Tshs 60,000 to Tshs 70,000. For teacher training education, the rise has been from Tshs 65,000 to Tshs 85,000. Women's enrolment as a percentage of the total enrolled has improved at the secondary education level, improving the gender balance. Form V female students' places have been increased from 663 in 1995 to 942 in 1998 (Ministry of Education and Culture, 1997/8).

The growth in educational provision from non-government sources has increased significantly. Pre-schools are estimated to have increased from 2,039 in 1995/96 to 2,335 in 1997/98, of which 68 percent belong to NGOs. Private primary schools have doubled, from 10 in 1995/96 to 20 in 1997/98. Private secondary schools have increased from 336 in 1995/96 to 369 in 1997/98, while in the same period, public secondary schools have increased from 259 to 416. As a result, the transition rate from primary to secondary grew from 7.3 percent in 1995 to 8.5 percent 1997/8. A new feature of the system has been the appearance of private institutions of higher learning, which did not exist before 1995 - by 1998 there were four private university colleges.

An action plan for transferring responsibility to local school committees has been prepared. The Local Government Reform Act of 1998 refers specifically to this change. A pilot project for decentralisation through a block grant system covers 35 Local Authorities. In principle, less developed regions/districts have been accorded preference when being considered for assistance to open new secondary schools.

The long period of decline in the enrolment rate in primary schools has been checked. The GER increased slightly from 77.6 percent in 1995 to 77.9 percent in 1997/98 (Mukyanuzi, 1999). Measures to improve the quality of education are still largely at the planning stage. A strategy has been adopted to co-ordinate resource centres and to implement action plans for the reform of technical and higher education. It is intended that minimum teacher qualifications will be raised (especially at the primary education level).

Performance of the health sector

The most significant change in health provision is the growth in non-government health care facilities, particularly at the initiative of health entrepreneurs. The total of 3,577 health facilities in 1995 had increased to 5,002 by 1998 (MoH, 1998). Out of the 5,002 health facilities, only 2,302 are government owned.

Cost sharing user charges have been introduced at all levels of the referral system, with fees depending on the category of the service. The government has recently approved proposals for a regulatory and institutional framework for health insurance in the formal sector. All public workers will have a percentage of their monthly salaries remitted to the health sector authorities.

Specific measures to improve health include action plans for malaria control, the raising of public awareness of HIV/AIDS, and the intensification of community awareness of hygiene and sanitation. Although there have been some successes (severe malnutrition has declined from 6 percent in the late 1980s to 2 percent in 1998), life expectancy has remained static at 50 years for the last decade, the IMR is still 92 per 1000 births, MMR remains at 200-400 per 100,000 births and the under-five mortality rate is 141 per 1000 births (URT, 1998/9).

Performance of the water sector
Access to clean water has stabilised, but no breakthrough has been achieved. In 1995, 50.5 percent and 68.3 percent of the rural and urban population respectively had access to safe and clean water within a 400-500 metre distance. By 1998, rural coverage had declined slightly to 49 percent while urban coverage increased to 81 percent (MoH, 1998).

There has been some improvement in sanitation, rural access increasing from 79 percent in 1995 to 84 percent in 1998 and urban access from 85 percent of households in 1995 to 97 percent in 1998. Beneficiary participation was promoted through the Participatory Hygiene and Sanitation Transformation programme (PHAST) which has been introduced in Kigoma, Mtwara and Dar es Salaam. Pilot districts included Ilala, Kasulu, Kigoma and Mwanza municipal council. Participants are trained and, in turn, train their respective communities in good water, hygiene and sanitation practice. This cascade approach should help the community to identify problems, priorities and visualise solutions. There has also been a training programme on the construction of special types of pit latrines in Morogoro and Dodoma Regions (MoH, 1997).

Community health workers have been given the task of promoting the formation of community/village level water, hygiene and sanitation committees. These committees have been given a PHAST manual translated into Kiswahili. In the areas where the programme operates, 40 percent of the villages are reported to have formed water committees and 28 percent have set up village water funds.

Some lessons and challenges

In the social sectors, government has had some modest success. Available indicators suggest that the declines in provision experienced since the early 1980s have been arrested, and in some areas there have been improvements. This period has also seen important policy changes, likely to profoundly change the social service delivery system. However, progress towards many stated objectives continues to be constrained by a lack of resources. The government continues to struggle to supply services and meet public expectations with an inadequate resource base. In some cases the operational content of general objectives, such as improving educational quality, has not been adequately spelt out.

In the coming period, the social service delivery system faces a number of difficult challenges:

(a) fostering local level management of public education, health and water facilities, which requires continuing development of human capacity and institutions to manage delivery at the local level;

(b) addressing issues related to the management of a more plural system, starting with a deeper analysis of the policy implications of the rapid expansion in non-government delivery systems;

(c) pursuing long-established and often repeated goals to increase access to social services; and

(d) addressing issues related to the quality of services.

Education

Implementation of some objectives will have to be extended over the long term. Decentralisation in education requires the strengthening of weak local government institutions, human resource development and clarification of the relationships between different levels of government (district, regional and central).

The devolution of power to plan and manage from the centre to the lower administrative levels (the district, the ward, the village, and the school) will involve a fundamental change in the allocation of responsibility and in administrative practice. Currently the Ministry of Education headquarters plans and controls activities in terms of human, physical and financial resource allocation, not only at the regional and district levels, but also at the level of the school. Over centralisation limits local initiative and undermines the independence and self-confidence of educational institutions. However, an improved system will have to be created with great care. From the point of view of school personnel, replacing bureaucratic control from the centre by control through a local bureaucracy will only be an improvement if the system of local government is effective in representing the needs of the local population and sensitive to requirements for effective schooling. An important role could be played by parents' committees, but many issues need to be resolved, such as how these should be constituted, what their powers should be and who they should be answerable to. Decentralisation demands the development of management skills by head teachers, parents' committees and local government officials and representatives.

The development of a pluralistic government/non-government delivery system does not absolve government of responsibility in the non-government sector, either in relation to monitoring quality or facilitating improvements in the performance of non-government institutions. The government could, for example, help private educational institutions tackle problems such as access to land, credit facilities, and lack of qualified teaching staff. The government could also ease bottlenecks in the procedures for establishing private schools, including the distribution of booklets regarding procedures for establishing schools. Estimates of teacher training needs should take into account demand from private educational institutions. The government could also consider grants to make up part of the salaries of private school teachers.

The government's shift of policy towards reducing its role in public service provision has been widely criticised and it has come up against pressure to continue funding services. The shift in responsibility for running secondary schools from the government budget has been diluted by the pressures on government to incorporate community schools into the public system, particularly in response to lobbying by members of the Bunge. However, scarcity of public resources means that most community initiated schools taken under the public wing still lack essential facilities. As a result of the government accepting responsibility for community-initiated schools, the earlier trend towards shifting the balance towards non-government secondary education has been reversed.

Despite verbal commitments to improve the quality of public education, there has been little progress. Examination results in government secondary schools (one measure of efficiency) have been poor for almost two decades, particularly when compared to the better long established non-government schools (mostly seminaries). Proponents of higher quality education argue that public schools need to retire inadequately qualified teachers and supervise and improve incentives to good ones, something the government has so far failed to do.

Realistically the government will be under continuing pressure to spread limited resources thinly. Older Tanzanians, who bemoan the passing of the halcyon days when Tanzanian secondary education was of a high quality, need to remember that thirty years ago the system was highly selective and elitist. A return to such a system would be politically unacceptable. There is likely to be ongoing pressure to expand places at secondary and post-secondary levels. This process has been observed during the current administration. Over 1995-1998 there was a rise in the transition rate (7-8.5 percent) of standard VII pupils to Form I in public secondary schools. However, qualitative improvement is still not being achieved.[27]

Secondary school selection is based on a quota system, which essentially allocates Form I places in accordance with the size of enrolment in a district/region, irrespective of whether pupils perform well or not. This practice removes the incentive to achieve a given pre-set national standard of performance. Equity considerations at Form V selection may also be pursued at the expense of standards (for example, reducing mathematics requirements for girls to achieve a more equal gender balance).

In considering strategic options to support a more pluralistic social service delivery system, the possible provision of credit facilities and public financial assistance to private institutions has been considered, but such ideas have yet to be implemented. Experimental efforts have been made to place funds for primary schooling more under the control of parents, to increase the element of choice, but no system has yet been devised which will be readily replicable on a national scale. Some problems remain intractable. Higher (post-secondary) education is expensive, claiming a disproportionate share of educational resources to benefit a small percentage of those in education. Nevertheless, in relation to expectations, the universities are under-funded and university lecturers see themselves as under-paid.

University students have not had to contribute to the cost of their education, while fees (at least Tshs 2,000) are charged for primary education. However, given the high cost of university education as compared to the average household income, the contribution the average student could make through fees would only account for a very small proportion of total costs. Setting fees at a level which could bear a substantial proportion of cost, without an adequate scholarship programme, would exclude most households from access. A loan system is one possible solution, but in the short term that would not contribute to real resource availability, as the loans would have to be funded. Whether a loan system would contribute to resource availability in the longer run would depend on repayment.

The achievement of universal access to primary education remains a fundamental goal. With less than 60 percent and 80 percent NER and GERs respectively, that goal is far from being achieved. Inevitably, when enrolment falls significantly short of universal, marginalised social groups such as the very poor, nomads, working children, girls, and HIV/AIDS orphans, are excluded.

Government goals are that by the year 2000, 85 percent of school age children should be in school, and by 2004 universal primary education should be achieved. To achieve that target, a concentrated mobilisation of effort is required now. Unfortunately, this seems unlikely to be accomplished in the near future.

Quality improvement objectives have also been set. Currently, passes at the standard VII examination are hardly 40 percent and those who score at least 50 percent constitute only about 15 percent. At the secondary level, less than 80 percent pass the form IV examination, two-thirds achieving only division IV. It has been proposed that an appropriate target pass rate at the primary level should be for at least 50 percent of the candidates to pass the standard VII examination and at form IV level the target should be for most candidates to score at least division III. The challenge is to attain these targets without a trade-off between quality and quantity. Past experience illustrates that it is difficult to extend coverage and improve quality at the same time and yet this trade-off is often overlooked in discussions about education policy in Tanzania.

The resource problem is clearly illustrated when the availability of funds is compared to ministry estimates of funding required to achieve a reasonable quality of performance. At the primary education level it has been estimated that there is a resource gap of 87 percent, at the secondary, teacher and higher educational levels, the gaps are 74 percent, 76 percent and 13 percent, respectively. When non-governmental financial sources are taken into consideration, the gaps are less. At the primary education level, the remaining gap constitutes 51.4 percent; at the secondary level 38.6 percent; at the teacher education level 63.6 percent, while at the higher educational level, it is only 9.4 percent (Mukyanuzi et al 1998).

Various proposals have been made to reduce the resource gap (such as the district council's levying an education tax on beer, spirits and cigarettes). Such proposals imply that there is some mechanism whereby the overall tax take can be readily increased to meet a specific need, or that tax revenues should be pre-empted for education by earmarking. The same sort of argument can be applied to any other high priority sectors. However, it is unlikely that efficient expenditure allocation would be achieved by circumventing the budgetary process by earmarking tax revenues to a specific use. The other option on offer is increased cost-sharing, that is, households using the service make a greater contribution, in addition to their tax contributions. Existing proposals suggest that at the primary education level the burden could be shared between government (66.5 percent), households (31 percent), voluntary contributions (1.5 percent) and community (1.1 percent). At the secondary education level, the relative shares proposed are government 36.6 percent, household 60.7 percent and school 2.7 percent.[28]

For those households with discretionary income, such proposals make sense. Many such households already make payments for private services, and it might be rational for them to contribute towards improved public services. However, it also has to be recognised that the underlying scarcity of resources reflects the reality that Tanzania remains a very low income country, and a large segment of households have little discretionary income, using their cash to meet minimal household requirements for food, shelter and clothing. For such families, increased cost-sharing would seek to transfer the cost burden to households that are unable to bear the burden and who will therefore not be able to access the service.

Possibly the main hope for an improvement in teaching standards lies in the increasing supply of educated teachers, in what has become a softer labour market. However, to take advantage of an increasing pool of potential teachers, there needs to be a transparent and fair system of removing incompetent teachers and recruiting on the basis of ability. A possible mechanism would be for primary teachers to be re-assessed, especially in English and Mathematics, at skill levels comparable to those tested in the standard VII examination. For those remaining in the profession, efforts are required to base promotion on performance. Teacher assessment could, in part, be based on student achievement in examination results.

A perennial problem affecting social service quality has been the lack of funding for non-salary inputs. In 1998 student per capita expenditure for non-salary items was Tshs 917 and Tshs 15,872 for a primary and secondary school students respectively, compared with a long term desirable goal of Tshs 34,294 and Tshs 56,567 respectively. Rationalising the use of teachers on the basis of official teacher student ratio norms could release some funds. Rationalisation would entail hiring on a demand driven basis and abandoning the supply driven approach of retaining all teachers. However, realistic assessment of future resource availability suggests that the government will continue to lack the funds necessary to cover the desired minimum expenditure on non-salary inputs.

At the higher education level, financial problems result from the high unit costs which range from Tshs 1.9 to 2.9 million, out of which Tshs 773,000 constitute students' direct costs. Most students receive government bursaries to cover these costs, whether they have the ability to pay or not, and whether or not the courses they pursue are of value to the community. This contrasts with the fact that households pay for the education of their children at all other levels. It is therefore proposed that higher education students should at least pay from their pockets Tshs 173,200 in respect of caution money, student union fees and stationery and book allowances. Payment for the remaining Tshs 600,000 could be made to a varying degree by the beneficiary, depending on the priority the government attaches to the course and the student's ability to pay. Government would need to set academic priorities against which to gauge what students should pay, and institutions of higher learning would need to apply a means test to assess their students' ability to pay. However, this may not be straightforward in Tanzanian circumstances, where students access to funds may be through the extended family.

Discussions within the government about strengthening the education system emphasise capacity building needed to strengthen skills in management and educational planning, and efforts to enhance the capacity and role of national level institutions responsible for developing and monitoring performance. At the same time, emphasis is placed on decentralisation and more effective consultation, with initiatives to strengthen local capacity being integrated with local government reform programmes and health sector reform. It is evident that the education system should seek to balance the interests of various actors (children, parents, the community, government, teachers), and that it would be desirable to develop the professional skills of teachers. A recent appraisal report for an educational sector programme (1999) identified a number of areas as important. The report suggested focusing on child teacher interaction at the classroom level, decentralisation, capacity building of central institutions for curriculum development and assessment, priority to equity (gender and poverty), resource allocation more consistent with priorities, effective monitoring of expenditure, enrolment figures and educational outcomes. The report emphasised that communication is essential - upwards, downwards and sideways.

While the educational ideas expressed in such reports appear sound, it seems less evident that many of the real problems of the education sector are being confronted. Choices between quantity (coverage) and quality are avoided by espousing commitments to universal primary education, an acceptance of a fast growth in secondary schools and achieving substantial improvements in quality. The expensive and elaborate superstructure of institutions to manage examinations, inspect schools and develop curricula, developed over the years with donor support, has been quite ineffective in the past in ensuring quality or even maintaining a minimum level of performance. Yet it is that superstructure which is expected to play the lead in future development. Perhaps most worrying, there seems to be an absence of in-depth evaluation by donors of previous failed involvement in the education system. Donor initiatives have contributed to increasing unit costs and the creation of unsustainable facilities in the past. To be more effective in the future, a more radical reassessment than has yet been attempted, will be required.

Health

The health sector is also under funded by comparison to internationally defined minimum norms. In 1998, per capita spending was Tshs 2,400 (US $3.5) per annum, compared the international norm of Tshs 8,400 (US $12). As with primary education, the size of the gap indicates that there is little chance for Tanzania to achieve an 'acceptable' level of expenditure on public health until a much higher national income is achieved. At current budget levels, the government would have to allocate around one-third of the total budget to health to approximate the norm, as defined by institutions such as the WHO.

The main financing source for the public health service continues to be the central government, with sources such as user-charges, insurance schemes, and community contributions constituting hardly 5 percent of recurrent expenditure. Moreover, available funding is still highly skewed towards tertiary hospital services and personal emoluments. Health expenditure figures indicate that about 77 percent of government resources are spent on curative services, while only 14 percent is spent on preventive services leaving 9 percent for administration. Most of the existing health facilities, especially at the lower level, are not adequately equipped with essential supplies. The relatively low budget share allocated to the low level health facilities does not permit adequate stocking of supplies (MoH, 1996).

Cost-sharing in the public health sector could be enhanced, depending on fee structure and quality of services provided, as is demonstrated by the willingness of quite poor households to pay for non-government medical services. An improved quality public service could attract more paying clients. Also health insurance and workers' health schemes could be developed. Formal sector employers could enter into agreement with facility managers to pay for the medical services of their workers. A contributory cooperative health scheme could also be developed for those outside the formal employment sector.

One underlying cause of high morbidity is lack of effective prevention at the household level, which relates to low levels of education and health awareness within the community. Efforts should continue to shift budgetary allocation towards preventive medicine and to low level health facilities, such as dispensaries (as opposed to district, regional and consultant hospitals). If dispensaries were well staffed and had adequate medical supplies, fewer patients would have reason to be referred to higher level facilities. Also, in health as with education, it would be desirable to shift the balance of expenditure away from personal emoluments towards the supply of other necessary inputs.

Nevertheless, there are realistic limits to the degree that resources can be shifted away from hospital facilities and personal emoluments for the more highly qualified staff. In a market economy, where doctors have the choice of internal and international mobility, their income expectations must be taken into account. Demand for curative services from the economic and political elite also places pressures on the system. It makes little sense not to fund local hospital facilities, when members of the elite are provided with access to medicine abroad at public expense, as has been the practice in the past. If expensive training institutions could become semi-autonomous and partially self-financing that could reduce government financial burden.

Unfortunately, the shift towards non-government health provision is not likely to address the health requirements of the rural population that currently lack access to services. The development of private services in recent years has been highly skewed to the urban areas, in particular Dar es Salaam.

Although primary health care has been a success, it has been highly dependent on programmes which are donor driven and managed. There is a need to increase consumer participation and to build capacity in the community to sustain primary health care. Consumers still tend to see primary care as a curative service, neglecting community efforts to promote preventive care. There is also a need to extend training and understanding of primary health care requirements among the higher level health service personnel. Local communities also need to be persuaded to pay for village level health services.

Participatory strategies (as incorporated in PHAST) provide an attractive alternative to more centralised strategies, but it will take an extended period to attain national coverage and realise the promise of the approach. The initial programme has only involved eight districts. The approach has proved expensive and the impact at the grass-roots level, so far, has been modest.

Water

Safe water supply is a crucial factor in disease prevention. Access to a safe water supply, however, is constrained by low management capacity of the water sector. Although in principle rural and urban water coverage was 49 percent and 81 percent respectively, in 1998, effective coverage in rural areas may now be as low as 30 percent, because several rural schemes do not operate at all. The solution lies in adopting technologies that are relatively easy to keep running and developing village level capacity to operate and maintain water facilities.[29]

3. Monetary policy and financial sector developments

Macroeconomic management is essential for stability, ensuring that a society lives within its means and for sustaining economic growth. An important tool of macroeconomic management is monetary and financial sector policy. This chapter examines monetary policy developments and financial sector reform.

Monetary policy developments

Monetary and credit policies under the Third Phase Government have been quite firm, aiming to subdue inflation and maintain positive real interest rates in order to promote domestic savings and ensure efficient allocation of financial resources.

Inflation

The 1995 Bank of Tanzania (BoT) Act increased the BoT's autonomy and strengthened its role in monetary management. The Act moved away from multiple central bank policy objectives to a single policy objective of price stability underscoring the commitment of the government to tackle inflation.

Tanzania has made progress in the fight against inflation. Over the period 1995-99, the rate of inflation has been decreasing (see Figure 2). The rate of inflation decreased from 31 percent in December 1995 to 15.4 percent in December 1996 as a result of the tight monetary and fiscal policies pursued during the period. The growth rate of M3 - broad money decreased from 32.4 in 1995 to 14.4 percent in 1996. There was a break in March 1997 when the decrease in inflation was interrupted; inflation rising from 13.8 percent in February 1997 to 17.5 percent in April 1997. Food shortage caused by adverse weather conditions was the main cause. However, as Figure 2 shows, the rise in inflation was not sustained for a long period. By December 1998, the rate of inflation decreased to 11.2 percent. By 1999 inflation rate declined further to a single digit reaching 6-7 percent in early 2000. Tight monetary and fiscal policies helped keep inflation under control in the wake of supply shocks.

To assess more accurately the effectiveness of monetary policy on inflation, one can use the non-food inflation rate. This measure leaves out the effect of food prices, which account for about 75 percent of the changes in the National Consumer Price Index (NCPI). Figure 3 below shows the behaviour of non-food inflation during the 1990s. Non-food inflation, which averaged about 26 percent during the first half of the 1990s started to decrease after 1995. It fell from 26 percent in 1995 to 22 percent in 1996 and further to 13 percent and 8.1 percent in 1997 and 1998 respectively. Inflation rate declined further to single digit level, and has stabilised at 6-7 percent.

Figure 2: Inflation in Tanzania 1996-1998

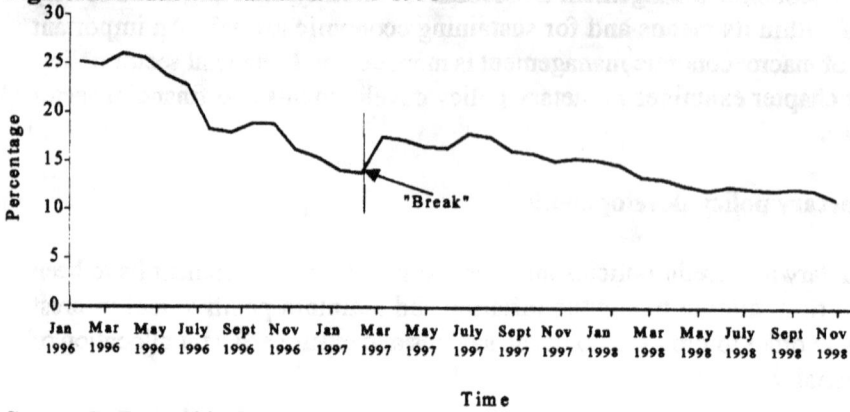

Time

Source: BoT Monthly Economic Review (various)

Figure 3: Non-Food Inflation 1994-1998

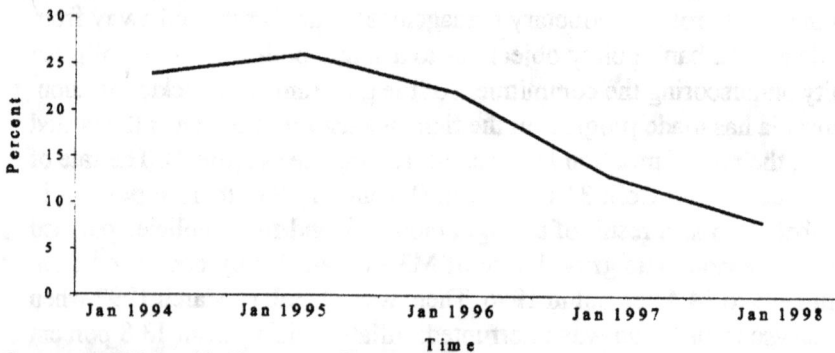

Time

Source: BoT Monthly Economic Review (various)

Prudent monetary and fiscal policies during 1995-99 have helped to bring down the rate of inflation. Supply shocks, and bad weather acted as setbacks, but non-accommodative monetary policy effectively prevented the escalation of inflation.

Interest rate developments
During the 1995-1998 period, interest rates continued to be market determined. Table 13 below shows developments of average deposit and average lending rates during 1995/96-1997/98. Both the deposit and lending rates declined over this period, but the interest spread was great. High interest spreads reflect a lack of competition, inefficient banks, high cost of doing business, inefficient market instruments and a high rate of loan default. While the real lending rate has been positive, the real deposit rate has been negative throughout the period (see Table 14).

Table 13: Development of Average Nominal Interest Rates

	1995/96	1996/97	1997/98
Deposit Rates	13.9	10.0	10.9
Lending Rates	33.8	25.8	22.0
Interest Spread (i.e. lending rate - deposit rate)	19.9	15.8	11.1

Source: BoT Economic and Operations report for year ended June 1998

Table 14: Real Interest Rates

	Year	Nominal Interest Rate	Rate of Inflation	Real Interest Rate
Deposit Rate	1995	21.0	29.8	-8.8
	1996	11.1	15.4	-4.3
	1997	7.3	15.4	-8.1
	1998	8.7	11.2	-2.5
Lending Rate	1995	34.0	29.8	4.2
	1996	30.0	15.4	14.6
	1997	24.3	15.4	8.9
	1998	22.0	11.2	10.8

Source: URT economic survey (1999)

Exchange rate policy

The main objective of the exchange rate policy has been to ensure the profitability of export production, by allowing the exchange rate to adjust to market conditions, with the government continuing to adopt a policy of minimal intervention in the foreign exchange market. Occasionally the BoT intervenes to stabilise the shilling, when it is felt the swing in the exchange rate is unacceptably high. However, large swings in fundamentals, such as large fluctuations in capital flows and food shortages sometimes make it difficult to avoid sharp short-term swings in the rate, given inadequate foreign exchange reserves (Ndulu, Semboja and Mbelle, 1998).

Investment and savings

Increasing the rate of investment and domestic savings are critical factors in promoting economic growth. Increased macroeconomic stability was intended to enhance domestic savings and the rate of investment. In 1997, with the objective of promoting investment, the government published a new Investment Policy Code (IPC), which attempted to address the weaknesses in the 1991 IPC.

However, the performance of domestic savings and investment has not been satisfactory. The ratio of investment to GDP, which in 1990-95, was about 25 percent decreased to 20.9 percent in 1996, and to 19.6 percent in 1997, recovering slightly in 1998. This rate has not been sufficient to sustain strong economic growth. One major reason for the decline in the investment ratio has been the declining trend in public investment. The savings ratio during 1996-98 ranged between 7 percent and 9 percent. This rate is very low compared to the average ratio for Africa (17 percent) and that for developing countries (24 percent). It falls far short of the levels which would be required to achieve the high growth objectives set out in the Vision 2025 document. Foreign savings have continued to finance most investments.

Financial sector developments

The National Bank of Commerce (NBC) replaced all private commercial banks operating in Tanzania following the Arusha Declaration of 1967. Following the enactment of institution specific acts that provided for their operation and regulation, four more state-owned financial institutions were established between 1967 and 1972. During that period there was an inadequate legal framework for supervising banks or enforcing prudent behaviour and this, combined with an unfavourable economic climate, led to a build up of bad debts. This, in turn, led to a deterioration in banking conditions in the 1980s and prompted the establishment of a Presidential Banking Commission (the Nyirabu Commission) in 1988, to develop recommendations for rehabilitating the financial sector. Following the commission's report, the government of Tanzania initiated a financial sector reform programme in 1991. The present financial structure is a consequence of reform measures that began around that time. The broad aims of these reforms were:

(a) to promote the mobilisation of domestic savings;
(b) to ensure the efficient allocation of financial resources;
(c) to promote competition and efficiency in the supply of financial services and to establish a framework for a healthy competitive banking system;
(d) to restructure the financial institutions to improve efficiency and the quality of assets;
(e) to popularise existing and new financial instruments;
(f) to establish secondary money and capital markets; and
(g) to provide a better flow of information to and from the financial market.

At the commencement of financial sector reform in 1991, the country's banking sector comprised six deposit-taking financial institutions. The banks were the NBC, which enjoyed a virtual monopoly on the mainland and extended credit to parastatals and the government; the Cooperative and Rural Development Bank (CRDB), the government's main rural banking vehicle, and, the People's Bank of Zanzibar (PBZ), a quasi-central bank to the government of Zanzibar. The non-bank financial institutions were the Tanzania Investment Bank (TIB), which provided development finance to the industrial sector; the Tanzania Housing Bank (THB), which specialised in rural and urban housing finance; and, the Tanzania Postal Bank (TPB), which mobilised deposits for investing in government securities.

In 1991 interest rates were liberalised and the Banking and Financial Institutions Act (BFIA) was enacted. The BFIA legalised the establishment of private financial institutions and gave the BoT the responsibility of licensing, regulating, and supervising banks and non-bank financial institutions. The Loans and Advances Realisation Trust (LART) was also created to facilitate the recovery of overdue debts transferred from state-owned financial institutions. The entry of private banks was permitted in 1992, but the first two - Standard Chartered and Meridien BIAO - did not begin operations until 1994. The 1995 BoT Act and a series of banking laws and prudential regulations, further consolidated the BoT's supervisory authority.

Before granting a license to an institution wishing to provide banking services, the banking supervision directorate is expected to analyse the soundness of its business strategy and financial position, its capital adequacy, the integrity and experience of the management, and its likely contribution to financial development of Tanzania. Minimum core capital requirements for commencing operations are Tshs 1,000 million for commercial banks and Tshs 500 million for non-bank financial institutions. In order to encourage the development of the financial sector outside Dar es Salaam, the statutory minimum core capital requirement is lower for regional financial institutions. Currently, the Kilimanjaro Cooperative Bank is the only regional financial institution in operation, but licenses to two more such institutions have been granted.

Since 1996, the financial sector has expanded dramatically. During 1997 and 1998 the Bank of Tanzania issued new licenses to four commercial banks. Two of these were the Bank of Malaysia and the First Adili Bank. The NBC, which prior to October 1997 controlled about 80 percent of commercial banking activity, was split into the NBC (1997) and the National Micro-finance Bank (NMB), initially continuing under government control pending their privatisation.

In May 1998 the government liberalised the insurance sector with the establishment of the National Insurance Board (NIB), also granting licenses to a number of private insurance companies.

By June 1998, the financial sector comprised 19 licensed commercial banks (17 operating), 9 non-bank financial institutions, 105 foreign exchange bureaux, and a number of informal intermediaries. Despite the large number of non-bank financial institutions and foreign exchange bureaux, the financial system is still dominated by commercial banks. Of the 17 operating commercial banks, only three, the NBC (1997), the NMB, and the PBZ, remain under government control. Combined, they still control 40 percent of domestic credit and 55 percent of deposits. The five largest banks the NBC (1997), the CRDB (1996) (created upon the divestiture of the CRDB in 1996), Citibank, Standard Chartered, and Stanbic hold 90 percent of all assets. The market share of the remaining 11 banks, which include foreign African, as well as indigenous Tanzanian banks, is only 10 percent.

Private banks operate almost exclusively in Dar es Salaam, maintain high minimum deposit balances, and lend primarily for short term trade finance, thus limiting their customer base to a handful of low-risk, high-value customers. Small and medium sized urban enterprises, as well as the rural population, continue to have limited access to banking services.

Efforts to restructure the NBC continued during this phase. In 1997, the government decided to divide the NBC, into two banks, the NBC (1997) and the NMB, and created a holding company to manage the residual assets and liabilities of the former NBC. A banking license was granted on condition that reporting to the BoT be intensified and performance benchmarks on profitability and credit quality achieved until the two banks were in compliance with the capital adequacy requirements mandated by the BFIA. The NBC (1997) was to focus on corporate and large business customers, and the NMB to be transformed into a micro-finance bank serving small rural and urban businesses. Both banks retained branches in the major urban centres, but most rural branches were assigned to the NMB. Both banks began operations in October 1997 under new management teams.

The NBC (1997) has maintained relatively high lending and low deposit rates to enhance its profitability, as mandated by its memorandum of understanding. Given its dominant position in the banking sector, its rates influence those offered by other commercial banks. As a result, the industry-wide spread between lending and deposit rates is high and deposit rates are negative in real terms, deterring financial intermediation. Interest rate spreads are expected to decline following the privatisation of NBC (1997) which should improve the mobilisation of savings and the allocation of credit to the private sector.

The Dar es Salaam Stock Exchange was established in April 1998, with the Tanzania Oxygen company being the first to be listed, followed by

Tanzania Breweries and Tanzania Tea Packers. So far it has been an elaborate exercise that has generated only very modest activity. No use has yet been made of the exchange by medium sized firms to raise risk capital. Too narrow a range of shares (currently only three) is offered for it to be attractive internationally as an emerging market, or to provide the basis for domestic investors to put together local share portfolios of any significance.

Achievements and challenges

According to Semboja and Killick (1998) "Tanzania has made major progress towards getting the macroeconomic fundamentals right and putting in place a general policy environment that is more favourable to private sector expansion and growth". Inflation has been brought down to a single digit level. Both the fiscal and balance of payments deficit have been reduced. The black market exchange rate premium has almost been eliminated. Effectiveness of monetary policy instruments has also improved. The creation of the Tanzania Revenue Authority (TRA) in July 1996 and the introduction of VAT in July 1998 increased the revenue collected. Along with improved government expenditure control, there was a reduction in the need to borrow from the banking sector. This was further aided by the fall in government subsidies to parastatals following the privatisation of many public enterprises.

However, even with improvements in tax administration, the revenue raised by government stills remains too low a proportion of GDP for the government to meet its basic recurrent spending requirements, let alone generate recurrent surpluses so as to contribute government savings to the development budget. Such basic requirements for effective government as adequate civil service salaries and proper funding of the operation and maintenance of donor funded projects will only be possible with a substantial increase in government tax revenue.

Future success in increasing government revenue will depend on the TRA further improving tax administration and on government measures to close tax loopholes. Excessive tax exemptions granted by government continue to limit the tax base, reducing the revenues available to government and raising the burden on those who cannot avoid meeting their tax liabilities.

Under the Third Phase Government, the reform of the financial sector has continued. The licensing of new financial institutions, the privatisation of the NBC and modernisation of the regulatory and supervisory environment in line with the Basle Committee's Core Principles for effective banking supervision have continued liberalisation and sought to ensure sound financial practices. The BoT is also closely cooperating with the central banks of Kenya and Uganda, the other members of the Monetary

Affairs Committee of the East African Commission, in harmonising banking supervision practices across the region. This is significant in light of the shock to public confidence following the collapse of the Meridien BIAO, which was taken over by the BoT after the failure of its parent company in 1995.

The main challenges still facing the government include:

(a) *Improving rural credit.* Even though there has been a number of financial institutions that have entered in the market in the last three years, many of these have been concentrated in Dar es Salaam.
(b) *Building public confidence.* There is a need to build public confidence in the banking supervision system, particularly in light of the Meridien Bank, Greenland and Trust Bank failures.
(c) *Improving competition and efficiency,* as most private banks operate almost exclusively in Dar es Salaam, request high minimum deposits and primarily cater for short term loans.

Competition across banks has remained low as each type of publicly owned bank caters for a specific customer type. Small and medium sized urban enterprises and the rural population continue to have limited access to bank services.

The performance of the multilateral donor institutions in the reform process has been mixed. The Nyirabu Commission had proposed an approach to the reform of commercial banking that would have involved dividing the NBC into three competing banks, all with national coverage. This proposal had been prepared after careful analysis, as the approach that was most likely to create a genuinely competitive banking system. The proposal was not supported by the World Bank and IMF, and as a result was not implemented. Later proposals supported by the World Bank to divide the NBC into three involved a proposal to divide its operations into three specialist, non-competing entities; the approach eventually adopted was to divide into two non-competing entities.[30] To develop an effective banking system, the introduction of more competition is essential, and it is unfortunate that the World Bank opposed the development of competitive public sector banking, which would have been an appropriate transitional step to the further privatisation of the banking system.

This Chapter highlights the importance of the private sector for the growth of the economy. It examines constraints on private sector development and evaluates the effect of the policy measures and facilities that the government has provided or failed to provide. Comparison is made between the government approach now and in past years.

Entrepreneurial constraints

Entrepreneurship and the role of elites
Tanganyika came to independence with little industry. The least developed of the three East African economies, it had a weak transport infrastructure and a minuscule graduate elite.[31] By comparison, Uganda had a much larger educated elite, better developed social and economic infrastructure and a fledging large scale industrial sector, based on colonial state enterprise (the UDC) and minority Indian capital. Kenya had by far the largest industrial sector in East Africa, owned by the large European and Asian minority communities and by multinational firms. Although not as large or important as in Kenya, the Asian ethnic minority communities played an important economic role in Tanganyika, and there has been a resurgence in their importance in Tanzania in the 1990s.

Tanzania moved towards a socialist development strategy with the implementation of the Arusha Declaration in 1967, a movement which accelerated in the first half of the 1970s, with the implementation of *Ujamaa* and of the basic industrial strategy. In relation to its connections with the international economy, post-Arusha nationalisation dislocated banking and other financial connections, and took most commercial services into the public sector. Policies both before and after Arusha displaced Asians from the trading sector, in which they had previously been major actors. The nationalisation of urban property further demoralised the Asians, as a result of which Asian emigration increased.

The African political and administrative elites were discouraged from property ownership and limits were placed on the development of African private business, which meant that in medium and large scale economic activity, foreign and minority community ownership was displaced by bureaucratic control. The Tanzanian technical elite was weak, and the attempt to develop the parastatal sector under a controlled and egalitarian incentive system proved unsuccessful.[32]

The liberalisation and privatisation of the East African economies under structural adjustment has not yet resulted in a significant influx of multinational companies. While no systematic study is available on new patterns of ownership, the impression gained from casual observation is that the main effect has been a resurgence of the Asian business community, not only in areas where they traditionally played a dominant role, such as trade, but in new areas such as banking and finance, and real estate development. The other significant change has been the entrance of South African business.

The resilience and persistence of Asian business in the face of expropriation, expulsion and restrictions on trade is quite remarkable. The presence of this active business community could be a source of strength, as well as a potential political irritant, for the future of all three East African economies. During the 1970s, with the diaspora of the Ugandan Asians, and the less dramatic migration of Asians from Tanzania and Kenya, East African Asians established themselves in the UK and North America and many business families now have connections there as well as in the Indian sub-continent.

In many East Asian economies, the overseas Chinese communities have played a strategic entrepreneurial role in their dynamic structural change. Could the Asian business community play a similar role in East Africa? One possible impediment to this proposition is the widespread resentment of the Asians, which made their expulsion from Uganda a popular political move throughout East Africa and renders their position politically fragile. However, in East Asia the Chinese immigrants have also been the subject of resentment and there have been incidents of extreme violence, yet they have still played a strategic role in development.[33]

Given the strategic importance of the Asian business community in the East African economies, it has been the subject of surprisingly little formal study.[34] A serious exploration of the potential role of the Asian business community, particularly in promoting export trade, is yet to be carried out.

New foreign actors in the economy
Another aspect of change in Tanzania, which is also observable in West Africa, is the active role of new entrants from other parts of the Third World. Particularly noticeable has been the engagement of South African firms following the end of apartheid. In mining, brewing and service activities (including hotels and banking) large South African businesses have become important players, and many small-scale entrepreneurs have also sought opportunities. There has also been interest shown by East Asian investors, including Malaysian involvement in banking, finance and communications, Thai involvement in gemstones, and Chinese investment in construction. Again, while these tendencies are clear from casual observation, they have yet to be subject to serious study.

A national business class?
A further question that may be posed relates to the impact of liberalisation

on the distribution of economic power and access to economic opportunities. One area of particular interest is the possible emergence of a national business class.

There are a number of reasons why this is important. Whatever the relative merits of a nation specialising in primary commodity trade, there can be little advantage in specialising in supplying labour, leaving the supply of capital, and all that goes with it, to foreigners.

There is also a political economy issue related to the development of a national business class. It is not so much a matter of the old Marxist debate about the importance of having a national rather than a comprador bourgeoisie, as the potential negative consequences of having a political and administrative elite without a stake in, or strong connections with, the economic elite.[35] Without some connection, the government is unlikely to be responsive to the needs of business, business will be susceptible to populist attack, and state functionaries could come to see business as essentially a source of rents.

Under structural adjustment, public employees have not done well, and the technical and administrative elite has, with some exceptions, fared badly. By comparison, a group of small scale business people that have emerged in such activities as trade, transport, mining and construction have done well in the market economy. Even in the professions there has been a burst of entrepreneurial activity, as health care and education are increasingly provided on a private basis.[36] However, with the demise of the parastatals in Tanzania it seems likely that African leadership in the large business sector will remain minor for the foreseeable future. Unlike Uganda and Kenya, where there are larger groups of African big business.

How can the emergence of African business be encouraged? This is a difficult and controversial area. In Asia the basic approach to the promotion of indigenous big business has been through one variation or another of 'crony-capitalism'; that is, the political regime favouring selected business groups through, either, explicit policies (Malaysian preferences for the Bumiputra under the NEP), or informal networks. Throughout the current crisis, crony-capitalism has received much criticism, and in the extreme cases of the Philippines under Marcos and the latter part of Suharto's regime in Indonesia, criticism seems well justified. Similarly, the crony-capitalism of the former Soviet Union does not seem to be proving beneficial to the economy. Nevertheless, successful participation in international markets is probably more likely with a developed group of national capitalists, and in the history of capitalist development this has typically involved an intimate relationship between the state and business. In order to encourage private sector growth the state needs to promote big business to the benefit of the national economy, rather than the Swiss banking system, or migration to the developed world.

The private sector and the policy environment

As seen in Chapter I, a spurt of economic growth during the ERP period has been followed by a period of more sluggish growth. The sectors that have had a significant impact on the pace of growth are agriculture, industry, mining and tourism, the performance of all of which largely depends on the private sector.

In its election manifesto for 1995 the ruling party, CCM set for itself the task of restoring, developing and protecting domestic industry and improving the privatisation process, seeking to:

(a)   encourage joint ventures between government and private investors (local and foreign);
(b)   promote employment creation;
(c)   encourage domestic resource use;
(d)   develop agro-industry;
(e)   encourage joint ventures for the development of coal; and
(f)   support SIDO to develop small industry, especially for women and youths.

After 1985, there was a steady increase in private investment (see table 11). However, there was decline in 1995-97, due to such factors as investor uncertainty about the effect of the 1995 elections and strained relations with donors. Private investment is reported to have declined from 20 percent of GDP in 1994 to only 12.5 percent in 1998 (Tsikata and Madete, 1999) although the decline was arrested in that year. According to Tsikata and Madete (ibid), Tanzania's private investment effort remains poor with both the quantity and quality of investment falling in the past five years.[37] The World Bank Country Economic Memorandum (1999) made the observation that private investment declined after 1994, probably reflecting the sharp decline in public investment.

The most important stimuli to private development are not specific measures to promote investment or to meet the needs of particular businesses, but the general environment of taxes, regulations and provision of public services. In the literature on transitional economies a good deal of attention has focused on the need for a level playing field between the private sector and state enterprises (i.e. state firms should not receive preferential treatment or subsidy). It is equally important that competing private firms should receive equal treatment; that there should be a level playing field within the private sector.

The policy and institutional factors that influence private investment fall into six broad categories:

(a) policies affecting economic conditions (e.g. the effect of fiscal and foreign exchange policies on the buoyancy of the economy);
(b) legal and regulatory measures (e.g. appropriate commercial, company and land laws);
(c) the division between private and public activities (e.g. ending inappropriate government monopolies and confinements);
(d) financial and other incentives to investors;
(e) provision of efficient economic infrastructure, where these are currently provided by government or state owned enterprises (e.g. roads, railways, ports, power, water and telecommunications); and
(f) the supply of trained personnel.

Economic Incentives

The previous chapters have given an insight into how the economic environment as a whole has changed for the better since the early 1980s. In the period of economic crisis, scarcities and an over-valued exchange rate made business very difficult (although there were segments of private business which thrived, particularly those which had privileged access to foreign exchange through import support programmes, and those firms which were adept in profiting from parallel markets). Improvements in macroeconomic policies affecting prices, trade, foreign exchange, inflation, fiscal performance, banking and interest rates have all contributed to an improved economic environment.

Focused efforts to promote specific private investments have been more problematic. The main instrument used by the government during the reform period has been the Investment Promotion Centre (IPC), established in 1991 under the 1990 National Investment Promotion and Protection Act (NIPPA), subsequently restructured and now known as the Tanzania Investment Centre (TIC). The aim of the IPC was to improve the investment climate and attract both foreign and local investors. A key instrument used by the IPC and TIC to attract investment is the provision of tax incentives.

However, there are problems with this approach. The first relates to the criteria for the allocation of incentives. On what basis should new investors be given benefits not enjoyed by existing firms with whom they may compete? Tax differentials unrelated to clear efficiency criteria introduce distortions into the incentive system. And what evidence is there that the benefits awarded stimulate investment, or are merely a subsidy to activities which would have happened anyway?

By March 1999, IPC/TIC had approved 1250 projects worth Tshs 2,779,662 million. Out of these, 598 projects were by local investors while 249 projects were by foreign investors and 403 projects were joint ventures. In terms of sectors, 627 projects or 50 percent were in manufacturing industries and 182 projects or 14.6 percent were in tourism. Three-quarters of the projects were new, while rehabilitation and expansion accounted for one-quarter. There is no available evidence, however, as to the net impact of the incentives offered; that is, which of these projects were the result of the incentives and which would have happened without any special inducement.

The issue of tax incentives and exemptions to new investors in Tanzania is a matter of controversy. Certainly the privilege of tax exemption was abused in the past. Exemptions and tax holidays contribute to the broader problem of excessive exemptions, which continue to result in a loss of revenue. International evidence suggests that tax holidays are not very effective in attracting foreign investments. A reasonable and stable tax regime, a predictable and non-intrusive regulatory system, good infrastructure and an effective supply of services are more important. Until recently, five year tax holidays were being offered to eligible investors. The period was later reduced to two years. In August 1999 Finance Minister Yona announced that the government intended to cancel tax holidays altogether.

It is important to understand that any tax concession is, in effect, a subsidy at the expense of other tax payers who have to carry the burden of the lost revenues - concessions for one group of businesses necessitate higher taxes for others. Such tax incentives become yet another exemption in a tax system that has been notoriously weakened by excessive exemptions. The record shows that any loopholes in the tax system are quickly misused to avoid taxes.

While low taxes may appear to be of benefit to individual businesses, in the long term they are of very limited benefit to the business community as a whole; if the country's revenue base is eroded too far the government becomes unable to fund essential services required for effective business operation.

Another concern, highlighted by past international experiences, is that the allocation of attractive tax concessions through bureaucratic discretion often becomes a source of corruption. Businesses interested in investment with a view to a long-term commitment are more concerned that the tax regime should be stable and not too onerous than they are with receiving short-term tax concessions. With the current state of public finances, tax concessions to selected investors should be eliminated. If there is a strong tax disincentive that should be handled by a general non-selective modification of tax rates for all taxpayers. The TIC should concentrate on promotion through publicity and providing a one-stop service to help investors through licensing procedures with a view to simplifying the investment process.

Legal and regulatory framework

Despite the improvement in the economy, there are still considerable weaknesses in the legal and regulatory framework and its administration. An attempt has been made to update some of the laws, but there is still much to be done.

One of the most important recent acts of legislation was the Land Act of 1998 based on the 1995 National Land Policy (NLP). This Act deals with land tenure, land use, access, land value, management systems, disputes, and the environment - aspects that are very important to private investors. However, this area clearly demonstrates that an effective legal environment is not only a matter of appropriate legislation, but also of effective administration of regulations and the law. Delays in getting title from the authorities, uncertainties regarding the validity of title due to lax administrative practices and difficulties (e.g. delays) in obtaining legal redress in asserting proper ownership rights all increase the cost and uncertainty of business.

Administrative services are not very helpful to investors. When it comes to the processing of documents through the bureaucracy, in respect of such things as business licenses and building permits, the administrative procedures can be very frustrating, particularly for those not versed in the tricks of gaining access to the bureaucracy. Bureaucratic delays have been a major problem in Tanzania. It has been reported that in Singapore, it takes only 15 minutes to process imports through the port; it takes 2 days in Namibia, South Africa and Mauritius; 3-4 days in Ivory Coast, while it requires 7 to 14 days with 10 pay-offs and 20 processing steps in Tanzania. Delays as long as 90 days have been recorded. To obtain a work permit in Tanzania you need 2 to 6 months and allegedly payments as high as US $5,000 have been made to obtain a work permit in 6 months. A building permit takes from 1 to 6 months. To get TTCL to install a telephone has been known to take anything up to 24 months; and power and luku (pay-as-you-use) installations from TANESCO are known to have taken up to 6 months. In 1996 there were 50,000 applicants waiting for telephone installation and 60,000 awaiting electricity connection. On top of these constraints it is also a common belief, within and outside Tanzania, that the country has one of the heaviest tax burdens in SSA when all taxes plus charges are considered. Therefore, the cost of starting and running a business in Tanzania is still too high when compared to many competing countries.

Restrictions on the use of foreign manpower, initially instituted to encourage localisation of the workforce, seem to have little effect protecting the local labour market but place costly demands on business people with a legitimate need to access foreign skills. By now, the natural protection provided by salary and benefit differentials and transport costs should provide sufficient protection to local staff. Government should critically examine the continuation of such restrictive regulations on the use of foreign personnel in a liberalised economy.

However, even in a liberalised economy, the government retains the responsibility to ensure that the private sector acts in a responsible manner in such areas as environmental protection, health and safety standards for consumers and workers, and physical planning to ensure that public services can be provided efficiently. The state should perform these functions by laying down clear policies and rules and enforcing them even-handedly, with proper constraints on official malpractice through the courts. Managing such functions is not easy, as it requires competence and probity among officials. Competence, because technical assessment is required in implementing regulations and probity, because in the absence of honesty, legitimate regulations can become simply a source of rents for officials, and rules can be by-passed by bribery. The present regulatory system is not only weak, but responsibility is scattered among various agencies with insufficient co-ordination to ensure the correct application of government regulations.

An important part of the legal environment is the maintenance of a high level of civil peace and order. Compared to the rest of East Africa, Tanzania has a good record of civil peace and suffers relatively little violent crime. However, the fact that the provision of private security has been a growth industry indicates that there is widespread concern about the security of property and weaknesses in police services.

One of the problems with the high degree of corruption exposed in the Warioba Report, is that it gives advantages to those able and willing to corrupt public officials. This not only causes a misallocation of public resources (e.g. by resulting in over-payments for services rendered to the government), but it also results in distortions in private business decisions. A corrupt environment discourages the entry of firms with high standards of business practice and service, and encourages the more dubious type of practitioner. Likewise, firms who honestly pay their taxes are placed at an unfair disadvantage compared to those who evade taxes by smuggling, corrupting tax officials and similar malpractice.

The appointment of the Warioba Commission by the President to investigate corruption and the publication of the Commission's report were significant and commendable steps by the Third Phase Government, but the Commission's report has not been followed by vigorous enough action to clear up the mess it exposed. See chapter 5 for further discussion of this point.

Division between public and private activities: control and liberalisation, nationalisation and privatisation

Under the Second and Third Phase Governments the changes which have had the greatest impact on private business came through liberalisation, which opened up important areas of economic activity such as agricultural marketing and international trade to the private sector, after more than two decades of public monopoly. Road transport (including urban passenger transport), has also been almost entirely shifted to the private sector. The process is continuing in such areas as shipping agency work.

The period 1967-1985
Following the Arusha Declaration in 1967 a large number of parastatal enterprises were set up, initially through nationalisation and gradually by creating new entities. It was felt that the private sector could not be relied on to provide the engine for self-reliant growth and that the public sector should be built up to play the leading role in development. Initially, following the Declaration, the performance of the parastatals was encouraging, the strategy seemed to have the potential to succeed and in the 1970s the parastatal sector was expanded vigorously. Donors (including the World Bank) lent their support through loans and grants to fund numerous parastatal projects. However, as the system expanded its performance weakened as the result of inappropriate political interference in key decisions (e.g. the location of plants in commercially unfavourable locations; the maintenance of pan-territorial pricing policies; under-capitalisation; the severe lack of experienced managers; and a deteriorating macroeconomic environment). Many parastatals became a financial burden to government and even with heavy subsidies they were unable to provide reasonable services to customers.

The First Phase government responded to the onset of economic difficulties in 1973-75 by intensifying administrative controls (e.g. over foreign exchange allocation) and tightening the regulatory system which acted to protect the state owned sector. The parastatals became increasingly dependent on treasury subsidy, privileged access to scarce foreign exchange and on external grants and loans to survive.

Initial attempts at reform in the early 1980s liberalised prices and allowed more competition with the private sector. This led to rapid increases in parastatal losses. Total government subsidy rose from Tshs 6.3 bn in 1984 to Tshs 50 bn in 1993, before tapering off to Tshs 21.8 bn in 1994. In addition, the parastatals were not able to pay dividends to the Treasury, instead demanding many tax and duty exemptions. A 1995 study by the World Bank, UNCTAD and COMSEC concluded that parastatal debt to the government by June 30, 1994 amounted to Tshs 689.1 billion, equivalent to 45 percent of GDP, of which 67 percent was foreign credit on loan to the parastatals.

The second phase policy (1985-1995)
The government embraced market reforms officially in 1985 under the ERP which had been designed in the final year of the First Phase government and implemented under the Second Phase government. It accorded the private sector an important role in the rehabilitation and development of the economy. To facilitate the transition from the domination by public enterprises a number of policy changes and initiatives were introduced, some of which have been implemented by the Third Phase Government.

In 1992, the government set up the Presidential Parastatal Sector Reform Commission (PSRC) to oversee the privatisation programme. Those enterprises that could not be reformed were to be closed down. The Loans Advances and Realisation Trust (LART) was given the responsibility of recovering whatever values could be realised from the assets of firms with non-performing debts to banks, either by sale of firms as going concerns or by breaking up the firms and selling the assets.

Divestiture objectives
The objectives of privatisation included: the generation of revenue for the government; development of broader share ownership; relieving the government from the financial burden of supporting these enterprises; and creating growth and employment opportunities through the more effective management of assets. Improvement in the use of under-utilised assets was expected to generate financial returns to the investors and tax revenues to the government. The broad modalities for public enterprise restructuring adopted by PSRC included the following:

(a) liquidation of enterprises considered to be non-viable;
(b) divestiture of viable enterprises via various methods (joint-ventures, outright sale, sale of shares, management and workers' buy-outs);
(c) lease of public enterprises or assets; and
(d) performance contracts for enterprises remaining under public ownership.

Implementation of privatisation under the Third Phase Government (1995-1999)
When the Third Phase Government took over, the divestiture programme

was moving steadily but not at the pace originally envisaged. Policy changes were introduced in 1996 to accelerate the process. The following table demonstrates the slowness of the progress achieved in the divestiture programme:

Table 15: Progress of Privatisation 1992-1999

Type of divestiture	1992	1995/ 96	1996/ 97	1997/ 98	1998/ 99*	Total **
Sale	5	24	25	29	7	119
Liquidation	0	9	11	6	1	60
Closure	4	7	1	0	0	14
Lease	2	7	1	1	0	24
Contracting	0	0	2	0	0	5
Others	Na	na	Na	9	4	7
Total**	11	47	43	45	12	279
Of which under LART	11	43	40	52	....	

Source: PSRC Annual Report 1997/8
Note: * Provisional figures
         ** Figures do not add up due to skipping of years

A number of positive results are beginning to emerge from the privatisation exercise in terms of investments, employment opportunities, profits and government revenue. Substantial investment in modernisation and rehabilitation has been made in some of the divested companies. One positive example is Tanzania Breweries, where investments amounting to about Tshs 32 bn. were injected in the firm by end of 1998. Losses incurred by TBL in 1993 and 1994 were turned into profit in subsequent years. Out of the profit obtained in 1998, the government has received Tshs 60 bn in dividends while taxes amounted to Tshs 24 bn. Consumers have benefited from a more reliable supply and improved quality. In addition, downstream employment in the distribution network has increased considerably. Other firms with positive results are TCC, Tanga Cement, Williamson Diamonds, ALAF and the Moshi Tannery.

In the 1998/1999 financial year it is estimated that the buyers of parastatals invested or committed to invest about US $136 million. A significant part of the foreign-owned profit has been reinvested locally. The total cumulative revenue generated from asset sales was anticipated to be around US $250 million and Tshs 32.6 billion. Of this amount the Treasury is receiving US $80 million.[38] Investors have pledged to invest a total of Tshs 30.2 billion and US $470.3 million in the divested enterprises.

The effect of the divestitures programme on parastatals not yet privatised has been mixed. TTCL, ATC, and TANESCO have achieved substantial improvements in operations. However, the long delays in privatising a number of parastatals such as the Kilimanjaro Hotel, has resulted in further deterioration.

Initial divestiture problems
A number of problems affected the initial privatisation process. The debt problem was foremost. Many debts had been accumulated by the parastatals to suppliers, banks and other government agencies, workers pension remittances, and foreign investors and lenders. The government did not have the funds to meet these obligations before passing on the enterprises to new owners. The second problem was dealing with the redundancy of employees, especially where the firm being privatised was not in a position to meet the termination benefits package. Another obstacle was the lack of enthusiasm among political leaders for dismantling the state sector, reflected in the behaviour of the bureaucracy. Resistance was reinforced in the case of some enterprises which had been acquired at great expense to the taxpayer which were sold for what appeared to be small amounts (even though commensurate with their actual value) to foreigners or Asian Tanzanians.

The problems for PSRC were complicated by the fact that crucial information about the enterprises was often missing or incomplete (e.g. on value of assets, liabilities, land titles, and operating strengths and weaknesses).

The new divestiture programme of 1996
Gradually many of these problems were overcome. LART took over the burden of dealing with enterprises that were seriously indebted. A decision-making impasse that occurred prior to and during the 1995 general elections was resolved in 1996, with the new government in place.

The cabinet adopted a new divestiture strategy in March 1996. Among other things it reiterated the government's strong support for the divestiture programme. It addressed the issue of benefits for retrenched employees. Above all, it articulated a strategy for the continuation of the restructuring and privatisation programmes for the remaining parastatals, including large public utility and infrastructure monopolies that could not be treated in the same way as the more straightforwardly commercial parastatals (e.g. water, power, telecommunication, railways, ports, and the airline).[39] These large organisations, most of which operate nation-wide networks, are politically very sensitive. Some of them will require a few years of restructuring and additional government investment before they can be made attractive to private investors. Out of the 385 firms earmarked for divestiture about 70 percent had been processed by end of 1998.

Criticism of the results: the indigenisation issue

Some people have argued that the implementation of the privatisation programme has been rather slow. In some cases the slow pace of privatisation has had very negative effects. A drawn out transition period can result in worker demoralisation, assets being vandalised and lack of planning for continuing operations. Others argue that the government has been too hasty in selling off enterprises, particularly those that are performing well, or are seen as strategic for the economy. Criticism is particularly sharp when firms are bought by foreigners, with the issue of indigenisation surfacing.

Government has responded to the call for indigenisation by exploring ways of empowering a larger segment of the population to take up shares or participate in private investment. It established the Privatisation Trust in 1998 to hold the remaining government shares in privatised enterprises and to work out suitable mechanisms for helping the wider public to participate in share ownership. It has commissioned a study on the issue of citizens' economic empowerment and is encouraging NGOs and banks to lend to small investors.[40] SIDO, NDC and other former holding parastatals are being restructured to play a more active role in promoting private enterprise. The government is also increasing its dialogue with private sector organisations such as the Chambers of Commerce and the newly formed Private Sector Foundation.

The performance of the government in managing the privatisation exercise and the reform programme has received some praise from donors. The contribution of the private corporate sector to the economy has not been spectacular but is rising steadily. A comparison between Tanzania and other countries in SSA shows that in implementing its programme of privatisation, the country has done fairly well. Research results published in the 1997 World Development Report concluded that privatisation in SSA had seen limited progress. The evidence suggests that Tanzania, Burkina Faso and Zambia have shown stronger political commitment to privatisation than many other countries in the region. Other features of that analysis are as follows:

(a) Apart from Nigeria, whose programme had stalled because of political stalemate, Tanzania had the largest number of enterprises earmarked for divestiture.

(b) Three to four year delays in effecting the privatisation programme have been typical in most countries.

(c) Tanzania was selling fairly small enterprises (a mean of US $2.76 million for 121 firms surveyed).

(d) The existence of a stock exchange was a useful facility in attracting buyers.

(e) The indigenisation issue has been universal, though more accentuated in Tanzania and Kenya than in other countries. In South Africa and Zimbabwe it has not been encountered precisely because the move towards privatisation has been hesitant for fear of the political reaction. The Wazawa in Tanzania bought only about 15 percent of the initial sale of 90 firms by end of 1995 (this number subsequently rose).

(f) Opposition to privatisation by employees has been a retarding factor. In Tanzania the issue has been considered in court several times, usually in favour of the government.

(g) In some countries, transparency in sale transaction has been lacking, leading to allegations of corruption. The privatisation process has not been one of the areas which has attracted charges of corruption in Tanzania. In Cote d'Ivoire, there were reports of nepotism ('privatisation of privatisation').

Provision of economic infrastructure

The other means by which the government supports private sector development is through the building and maintenance of the economic infrastructure. Efficient and competitively priced water, electricity, telecommunication, transport and financial services are crucial, both in ensuring the successful performance of existing businesses and in attracting foreign private investment. Low cost and efficient services are more important incentives for investors than tax exemptions.

In this regard, the Tanzanian environment is not very positive. In recent years, a serious discouragement to business and to investment has been the uncertainties resulting from inadequacies and disruptions in the supply of public services - water, power, and rail transport have all been seriously disrupted at one time or another. Also, Tanzanian telecommunications have never been at a level appropriate for efficient business and electricity costs are the highest in the region.

Some progress has been made on a number of fronts. Under the Second Phase government, with the support of a number of donors, substantial rehabilitation of the trunk road system was implemented. During the current administration, new power capacity has come on stream, which has basically improved the power supply situation. There has also been a significant improvement in telecommunications. The introduction of competitive mobile phone services has increased the capacity and flexibility of the system and there have been steady improvements in the capacity and reliability of the conventional phone system. The development of business internet services, while not placing Tanzania on the frontier of modern technology, has provided reasonable access to the worldwide web. However, Tanzania still has one of the lowest telephone densities of the SADC countries. And although there are six mobile cellular and paging services operating in main urban centres, with three companies operating pay-phone services in Dar es Salaam, the public owned telephone company still has a monopoly over land links and international telecommunication services. Overseas calls remain very expensive compared to rates available in most industrial countries, and the official monopoly has been used to restrict access to much cheaper international call-back services. Further liberalisation of the telecommunications market could be a useful step towards improving efficiency in the Tanzanian service sector.

Underlying potential of the informal and small scale sectors

The potential of the informal sector to absorb the unemployed and as a setting for training small entrepreneurs needs to be exploited more successfully. Policy should encourage small scale economic activity rather than harassing petty traders, as is often the case. And graduation from the informal to the formal sector needs to be facilitated with better access to credit, formal training, helpful tax incentives and a more facilitative regulatory regime.

Small scale enterprise has contributed to a number of sectors such as trade (much of the food trade is in the hands of small traders), transport (including the basic system of urban transport - the dala dala), building, and a wide range of craft and small scale repair and manufacturing activities. However, there are still very weak linkages between the small scale and larger scale sectors, with very little development of sub-contracting. Those in the informal sector face challenging bureaucratic hurdles to establish and run businesses in a more formal fashion. Most are concentrated in commerce and trade and are dominated by the young (20 to 30 year olds), according to the 1995 Dar es Salaam Informal Sector Survey. Most small enterprises have poor access to banks and to the more sophisticated marketing outlets; over 95 percent of financing for small enterprises comes from personal resources and family and friends.

In the past, SIDO and various other institutions have provided funding and support, but such support has typically serviced a very limited group of small businesses, and has not been very successful. It seems difficult for bureaucratic institutions to reach out to small businesses located in the poorer neighbourhoods and using the simplest technology. Some NGO efforts may be more successful in providing some technical assistance, but there is no coherent body of public policy or programmes to promote small- and micro-business.

Promotion of the private sector through capital markets

Three institutions have been established for the development of a capital market, that is a market for share-holding and other forms of investment in businesses. Under the Capital Market and Securities Act (1994), the Capital Market and Securities Authority (CMSA) in 1994, the Dar es Salaam Stock Exchange (DSE) in 1996 and the Privatisation Trust (PT) in 1998 were set-up. The CMSA is a regulatory and policy-making entity, charged with promoting and developing the equity market, regulating licenses for dealers in securities and establishing collective investment schemes. The DSE oversees the trading in shares. The PT is to hold in trust government shares in businesses that cannot be sold after an initial public offering. The CMSA had, by June 1999, licensed 12 dealers and 7 brokerage firms. The DSE was opened in 1997 with an initial public offering of TOL shares. A more successful sale was made in 1998 with TBL shares.

Participation in the stock exchange is still very limited. The market is far too narrow to make any significant impact on the economy or the asset portfolios of investors, and the volume of transactions is too trivial to justify the costs of the regulatory structure. The CMSA in collaboration with the PT has been studying the possibility of establishing collective investment schemes to broaden popularity of share ownership. But this is only likely to be successful when a much wider range of firms are listed in the market, including existing medium sized private businesses.

Challenges ahead

The development of a free market in Tanzania has been consolidated by measures taken during the Third Phase Government. Yet the task of promoting the institutional framework and improving the economic environment is far from complete. The efficiency of the tax system should be improved, so that it is fairer and the burden on those who pay can be reduced. Steps need to be taken to ensure that local government authorities do not impose an undue tax burden through local levies. Unnecessary regulations should be scrapped and administrative procedures speeded up. Economic infrastructure should be maintained in order to avoid costly disruptions in service. The legal framework should be modernised and administered so as to establish a more effective rule of law.

Generally, mistrust between the public sector and private sector needs to be minimised. The government and its agents have gradually improved their understanding of the role of the private sector, but business people still complain of slow, unpredictable and corrupt procedures. In some areas, private business people may not appreciate the necessary role of the public sector - perhaps understandably given the frustrations they have encountered with bureaucracy.

Structures also need to be developed to ensure better service from public utility monopolies such as water, telecommunications and electricity; they need to be made more responsive to client requirements, and held to higher standards of performance. Increased efficiency is needed in the final stages of the privatisation process. The period of transition from state controlled to private status should be reduced drastically and more effective control exercised over enterprises earmarked for privatisation to avoid the running down of assets. Examples of excessive delays include Kilimanjaro Hotel, Sungura Textile and Tanganyika Packers. Transparency in the divestiture should be ensured through the publication of the details of completed deals.

While the main thrust of policy should be in the direction of liberalisation, there are areas where there will be pressures for interventions. The issue of indigenisation has led to proposals to open up the ownership of shares and businesses to a wider public. However, that should not become an excuse to subsidise particular interest groups with access to the system, but rather suggests the need for measures to encourage greater indigenous entrepreneurial activity in an open and competitive environment.

Foreign investors will be attracted through measures to improve labour productivity, economic infrastructure, and efficiency in the processing of investment applications, more than by discriminatory tax concessions. Improvements in the workforce will require a persistent effort to improve training in technical skills and science based disciplines.

The Third Phase Government has made governance, the rule of law and fighting corruption priority issues.

Governance goals include:

(a) widening participation in decision making at all levels of the government;
(b) broadening democracy through better electoral processes and institutions;
(c) increasing access to information and knowledge;
(d) enhancing accountability of officials;
(e) protecting the weak and minorities; and
(f) promoting the rule of law to guarantee a secure and predictable environment for life and work.

Democracy and elections

The Third Phase Government came to office amidst a major transformation towards multi-party democracy. After the constitution was amended in 1992 to end the CCM monopoly, the first multi-party elections were held in 1994 and 1995. Though the ruling CCM Party won with a large majority, the opposition established a significant presence. Since 1995 there have been five political parties represented in Parliament out of thirteen that were originally registered.

Since the 1994 and 1995 elections, CCM has gradually regained ground, mainly as a result of squabbles in the ranks of the opposition and the opposition's failure to offer convincing alternative policies. In Zanzibar the opposition claimed it had won the presidential election, a matter that almost paralysed the political system in the isles. The Union Government has been indecisive in relation to Zanzibar, finding itself unable to influence events on the island or explain its apparent impotence. The Third Phase Government has inherited that conflict and other union problems. Many such issues are awaiting resolution and may be addressed in revisions of the constitution currently being prepared. Movement towards a solution of the Zanzibar conflict was not facilitated by the Commonwealth Secretariat until the middle of 1999.

In addition to problems relating to the political processes, four main issues in economic management require resolution between the Union Government and Zanzibar:

(a) mobilisation and allocation of external financial resources;
(b) payment and transfer of tax revenue, levies and charges;

(c)   appointment of key officials in economic management positions;and
(d)   foreign trade administration and external economic relations.

The media and information

There has been an impressive opening up of the media and a rapid expansion in communication facilities over recent years. There has been an explosive growth in newspapers, both in Kiswahili and English. Tanzania now has a totally free, lively and in some instances, scurrilous press. The better papers are beginning to develop skills in investigative journalism and the press has become an important social asset in informing the public and demanding official accountability. Television news reporting is also developing, although there is still little critical presentation or in-depth investigative work.

Within the period of the Third Phase Government, the state machinery has responded to the fast growing media with good sense, accepting the freedom of the press and making government information accessible to those seeking it. The rapid development of IT has led governments in many countries, including Tanzania, to liberalise IT and information exchange. In the early 1970s, the import of computers in Tanzania was strictly controlled. At that time there was only one main frame computer in the country (at the Treasury) and three smaller computers at Mwadui, TANESCO and the University of Dar es Salaam.[41]

Tanzania is now experiencing a boom in IT, with an increase in computer training courses, the widespread availability of computers and increasing access to internet facilities. In the June 1999 budget session of Parliament, the government recognised the value of this revolution by slashing import duties on computer hardware and software from 20 percent to 5 percent. The expansion of new media and the IT revolution have equipped society with the means to access and benefit from international information.

Advances in education and literacy levels, despite recent setbacks, have enabled the majority of the population (who cannot afford access to IT and other new means of high technology communication) increased access to written information. However, the effective use of literacy will depend on an expansion in the availability of reading materials, particularly inexpensive publications in Kiswahili.

Accountability and transparency

Corruption spread in Tanzania in the late seventies, in the context of an over-regulated economy, with scarcities in officially allocated commodities and a rapid erosion in the real value of official salaries. Larger scale corruption spread during the Second Phase Government, when lax management and dubious deals at the highest levels of government proved themselves to be the dirty side of economic liberalism which characterised that regime.

Upon taking office in 1995, President Mkapa boldly declared war on corruption and underlined the importance of government accountability and transparency. Upon his assumption of duty, President Mkapa appointed Judge Warioba to head a commission to investigate the extent, but not cause, of the problem. A nine hundred page document, the Warioba Report, produced enough evidence to show that corruption was widespread in Tanzania among government officials, politicians and the law courts. It recommended actions be taken to raise ethical standards by improving legal systems, laws and codes of conduct.

There are many forms of corrupt practices, often difficult to detect, arising both from need and greed. When left unchecked corruption becomes institutionalised, characterised by a deterioration in the value system, and public perceptions of norms of behaviour. Institutionalised corruption reflects gradual deterioration in the public value system as dubious practices become increasingly tolerated. It results from weak public policies which combine regulations that create possibilities of 'rent-seeking' by officials earning inadequate salaries. Ironically, under a completely defective bureaucratic regulatory regime, corruption can act as a greasing mechanism - using 'market' payments to bypass irrelevant rules and help the system function.

Examples of corruption which have impeded development include:

(a) inflating costs of projects and services delivered to public and private institutions;
(b) encouraging projects of doubtful value or economic priority;
(c) undermining the revenue collection efforts of the government;
(d) acting as a disincentive to genuine investors, while attracting those with dubious intentions; and
(e) subverting the regulatory functions of government.

All of the above acts were identified in the 1996 report on corruption in Tanzania by Judge Warioba. The main steps the Third Phase Government has taken to fight this corruption are:

(a) The formation of the Warioba Commission (Presidential Commission of Inquiry against Corruption).
(b) President Mkapa instructed all ministries, regions and public institutions to study the Warioba Commission Report with a view to

implementing its recommendations in their respective workplaces.

(c)   Following the recommendations of the Warioba Report, a Task Force was formed under the Prevention of Corruption Bureau to investigate high level officials associated with corruption, as presented in the Warioba Report. Action was taken against some culprits, including legal action, dismissal or retirement in the public interest.

(d)   A consultancy team headed by Judge Warioba was formed to follow up the implementation of the Warioba Report in ministries and other public institutions. The team consulted with ministries regarding reports submitted in response to recommendations of the Warioba Report. The report was presented to the President in January 1999.

(e)   The President appointed a minister of state in his office responsible for good governance.

(f)   In October 1998 the President instructed Regional and District Commissioners to conduct public hearing in all wards.

(g)   Civil service ethics and regulations were reviewed and various measures taken to enhance performance, including improvements in working conditions and salaries.

(h)   Regulations and procedures for procurement have been reformed to enhance accountability and transparency.

(i)   Tax exemptions have been checked and the role of the TRA in this respect has been made more explicit. Transparency has been enhanced by having exemptions presented to the Parliamentary Standing Committee on Legal and Constitutional Affairs for scrutiny.

(j)   TRA's tax administration programme, Customs Reform Programme, Pre-shipment Inspection Programme, Tax Payers' Education Programme and Tariff Harmonisation between the Tanzanian mainland and Zanzibar have been implemented to enhance accountability and transparency.

(k)   The Judicial Service Act of 1962 has been amended to facilitate supervision of Magistrates by the District and Regional Judicial Boards. Regulations governing court brokers have been reviewed. Judicial ethics committees have been established at district, regional, zonal and Court of Appeal level.

(l)   Immigration procedures have been streamlined. The department is allowed to retain part of the revenue collected to help finance the Immigration Department Reform Programme.

(m)   The Land Bill (1999), the Professional Surveyors Registration Act No. 2 (1997) and the formation of the National Council of Professional Surveyors aim to curb corruption in land matters.

(n)   The Prevention of Corruption Act No. 16 of 1971 was amended in 1997 to restore legal powers of arrest, detention and entry and search of the

PCB.

(o) The National Anti-Corruption Strategy and Action Plan for Tanzania (1999) has been produced, guided by the principles of prevention, enforcement, public awareness and institution building.

In the meantime, Transparency International, in its annual report of 1998, ranked Tanzania as one of the most corrupt nations in the world, placing it in the same league as Nigeria. In 1999 Transparency International repeated the same allegation. In fairness, knowledgeable observers question the methods used for ranking. While there are no grounds for complacency, it is not evident that corruption is so ingrained as to justify Tanzania's promotion to first division in the international corruption league. Indeed, the readiness of the government to publicise scandal illustrates the government's willingness to bring the issue of corruption into the public domain. All of this exposure has created the impression of a sudden epidemic in corruption just as the government has begun to seek ways of tackling the problem.

The issue of corruption is by nature controversial, but there is now widespread public recognition that the situation is very serious and needs urgent action. Eventually, government will have to take more decisive action to punish those guilty of corruption, no matter how senior they are. In many ways Tanzania is a small society, and instances of corrupt behaviour become well known among the general population. The government's continuing credibility will depend on it being prepared to take a much harder line with corrupt individuals than it has so far been willing to take.

A number of additional steps could be adopted to stem corruption and enhance transparency within the government:

(a) replacing discretionary powers of government agents by standard rules and procedures, and making this information widely available to the public;

(b) avoiding excessive rates of taxation that induce risk-taking by dodgers and defaulters;

(c) simplifying government procedures related to delivery of public services, fixing a maximum period for processing documents and delivering specific services, and requiring departments to propose annual targets or benchmarks for evaluating progress;

(d) improving personnel management policies to reward good performers;

(e) increasing the visible political commitment in combating corruption;

(f) providing amnesty to previous offenders, while instituting a new code of conduct that is rigorously enforced through tough legal sanctions;

(g) establishing greater disclosure of government procedures in handling finance, awarding contracts and making important appointments; and

(h)   subjecting military procurement to disclosure after a specific period.

Public service

A civil service reform programme was launched as early as 1991. It was intended to respond to the need for a new style of administration resulting from the withdrawal of the government from direct production and micro-management of the economy, to restore the effectiveness of public administration after a long period of decline and to reduce public employment. The reforms gradually cut back the civil service force to more affordable levels. Ministerial structures were rationalised by reducing the number of divisions by as much as 25 percent between 1992 and 1997. The government labour force shrunk from approximately 355,000 to 27,000 during that period after three retrenchment exercises.[42] Currently the social services, police force and the local government constitute the bulk of the public service. And despite earlier efforts to tighten up management of the civil service, it was reported in Parliament in June 1999 that recently the government discovered 3,184 ghost workers.

One weakness of the programme to slim down the civil service is that it was implemented partly through a freeze on recruitment, with many redundancies based on the 'last in - first out' principle (it being more expensive in the short-run to retire longer serving officials). This has resulted in an ageing of the civil service - a process that will be reinforced by the decision to raise the official retirement age from 55 to 60 years. This is unfortunate, as a steadily ageing public service is not likely to be the most responsive to innovation.

Another outcome of reform was an increase in civil service pay to reasonable levels. Salaries were increased from an average of Tshs 12,000 to Tshs 54,000 per month during the period. Unfortunately, the real value of salaries was still too low to act as an effective incentive for raising productivity and efficiency in the public service, but reflected the reality of fiscal constraint. Salary changes were combined with an effort to make the payment system more transparent, by incorporating many fringe benefits into the basic salary scale. However, the initial impact of that reform was to reduce the real net incomes of top civil servants, despite increases in nominal but taxable pay to compensate for the loss of fringe benefits. Thus in net terms the salary scale was further compressed (i.e. the range over which incentives could be offered at the middle and higher levels of the service was in effect reduced).

A further Public Service Reform Programme (PSRP) was formulated in 1998 for the period 1999-2004. This aimed to build on what was achieved in the previous period and to significantly improve performance. Objectives include improving discipline, developing clear lines of responsibility and accountability and generally introducing modern management principles and techniques. In May 1999 the President announced significant salary increases. Salaries were raised for the monthly minimum wage from Tshs 30,000 to Tshs 35,100 and the highest salary raised to Tshs 800,000. This package represents a significant move towards the decompression of the salary structure, to improve incentives at the middle and higher levels of the service.

A key objective of administrative reform is improvement in the budgeting system to reduce waste and relate expenditure to real activities and targets. This has been a stated objective of many government programmes over the years - a donor supported programme to introduce programme and performance budgeting was first implemented thirty years ago, and during the past decade there have been a number of TA programmes supporting improvement in budget management. Currently, a key component of the reform programme is the effort to improve the basic government accounting system, through strengthening the Accountant General's office in the Treasury and creating an effective system of control throughout the government system.

Completion of the current PSRP is scheduled in three phases over twelve years. Given the complexity of the task, this time span may be understandable but there is a risk that such a long time frame may reduce pressure to implement difficult reforms. Civil service reform has already been on the government agenda for about eight years. Many reports have been written and studies made, but a commensurate improvement in the public service has not occurred.

It is fair to say that improvements are being implemented in the management of the civil service and the organisation and operation of ministries, but it is far from evident that any breakthrough has been made towards the transformation of the civil service into a modern, high performance government machine.

Participation and local government reform

A proper dispensation of political and economic power to the people should be founded on democracy at the lower levels of government; at the village, ward and district levels. Theoretically, at those levels, it should be possible to have direct knowledge of local problems and through elected representation the concerns of stakeholders should have a direct bearing on policy. Yet, in practice, it is at the local government level where the inefficient discharge of government duties has often been most bitterly felt. The reasons for this situation are manifold, but the key ones are the following:

(a) lack of manpower capacities;
(b) insufficient financial resources; and
(c) ineffective systems of political representation, often resulting in dysfunctional interference in professional matters.

As a result of the above problems resource allocation does not always respond to the genuine priorities of the local electorate. Appointment of staff is not based on qualifications or experience. Job descriptions are lacking and rationale for staffing is rarely documented. At village and ward levels, often there are no offices or even very basic equipment. Staff are not only poorly motivated, they are also likely to be corruptible and ineffective in delivering services or collecting revenue.

However, it may be a mistake to place too much responsibility for weakness on the elected local authorities. Local government did not exist for an extended period following the dismantling of the district councils in 1972, and when they were re-established in 1984 they had only limited responsibilities because of the duplication of powers with regional administrations. Moreover, under the Local Government Service Act of 1982, the district authorities had very little control over a large number of their staff. The terms of service and appointment of many officers were controlled by the Local Government Service Commission, based in Dar es Salaam. An officer suspected of embezzlement could not be removed by local authorities without the approval of the Commission, a minister or the President.

Criticisms resulted in amendments to the Act in 1996 and again in 1999, leaving only the appointment of heads of department outside the control of the local authorities.

However, even if greater responsibility is handed to the councils, the problem of financing local government remains. They still depend on central government subventions (up to 80 percent for their recurrent needs and almost 100 percent for their development needs). Local government development projects are poorly formulated and supported by inadequate documentation. Lack of prioritisation of projects and scarcity of funds result in allocation of too little money to projects to facilitate project implementation and efficient running of services. During the recent decentralisation initiatives staff were arbitrarily transferred to district councils without due regard to the financial capacities of these councils (in the case of teachers, the exercise had to be suspended). The issue of division of responsibilities between central and local government in revenue collection has to be resolved; at present there is no clear-cut division of taxing jurisdiction between the central and local government (Report of the Task Force, 1999).[43]

Central government control major tax sources leaving local authorities with residual taxes that cannot generate adequate revenue (Report of the Task Force, 1999). Local governments levy industrial produce cess (city service levy in Dar es Salaam), agricultural produce levy, and development levy. The Task Force recommended that additional revenue sources should be transferred to local government (e.g. registration fees for medical services, slaughter and meat inspection fees, and registration of town commuter buses). For some other taxes, the share going to local governments should be adjusted upwards (e.g. hunting fees, land rent, forest royalty, court fines and mineral royalty). They also recommended that the industrial produce cess should be replaced by a service levy based on 0.3 percent of turnover, and proposed maximum rates for agricultural produce cess.

The policy management process

The Third Phase Government has initiated and approved many sectoral policy reports and proposals. Examples of areas in which policies were formulated include:

(a) Industrial policy (approved in 1996)
(b) Mining policy and strategy (approved in 1997)
(c) Initiatives for Mtwara development corridor
(d) Fisheries policy (1998) addressed small scale fishing needs
(e) Forestry policy (1998) and bee keeping (1998)
(f) Tourism Master Plan and tourism policy
(g) Agricultural Sector Policy and Sector Management Programme (1997)
(h) Investment policy (1997)
(g) Privatisation policy
(i) Civil service reform
(j) Telecommunications policy

The range of policy formulation has been quite comprehensive. If criticism is to be offered it is that there has been an output of policy documents that has been in excess of the government's capacity to implement. Many reports on policy include long lists of proposed actions, but fail to suggest a clear sense of priorities that focus on what realistically can be achieved under existing administrative and financial constraints. In addition, integration of all these policies in a common national framework has not always been ensured. Ideally all the policy documents were supposed to be guided by Vision 2025, but mechanisms to ensure this happens have not always been effective. This has undermined the integration of some of the policies and led to a gap between rhetoric and action.

A more effective implementation monitoring system is required to follow up government decisions and promises made to the people. While key monitoring needs to be done at the cabinet level, an independent entity selected from outside the government might provide complementary support.

Problems of refugees and affected areas

Tanzania has many neighbouring states, which have at one time or another experienced social instability, often generating a flow of refugees. The number of refugees has been high over many years, sometimes running into the millions (e.g. in 1994). The refugee population is at present estimated at around 800,000, although only 350,000 are living in refugee camps and special settlements. Because of their urgent need for food, shelter and medicine, they divert resources from the Tanzanian government and the donors that might otherwise have been used for development activities for Tanzanian citizens. Costs extend to environmental damage, congestion of social service facilities and deterioration in security. In some areas the host communities have had to abandon their homesteads because of security concerns.

The cumulative impact of the problem is serious. This would be the case in any country, but in light of the resource constraints facing Tanzania the burden is particularly great. The successive governments of Tanzania have had an impressive record of international solidarity in supporting refugees and have received external assistance. The burden continues, and there is little Tanzania can do to tackle the root causes except to offer its good offices for mediation where that might be effective.

There is some maximum carrying capacity of refugees in host communities, beyond which it becomes irresponsible to continue receiving refugees. In addition to welfare costs, the government is obliged to strengthen its police and security forces in refugee areas to give better protection to its citizens. For the country as a whole the strain on resources is never fully compensated for by international aid. If the burden is not adequately shared by the international community, the point may come when Tanzania has no choice but to put limits on the number of refugees it allows in and the duration of its contribution.

Challenges ahead

Three important broad governance areas present special challenges to the Third Phase Government: (i) implementing a clear vision of the role of government in development, (ii) solving the problems of the Union between the Mainland and Zanzibar, and (iii) completing the decentralisation programme. But alongside these grand issues, there are a number of more modest, but important and practical issues, which need to be tackled.

Reducing government waste

Outstanding national commitments should be reviewed to eliminate expensive activities no longer deserving priority. Examples might include creation of new administrative headquarters, the transfer of the national capital to Dodoma, the size of the security forces, financial support to political parties, discretionary and non-standard personal entitlements for sick and retiring officials, and external representation. National dialogue is needed to agree on identification and the reduction of such programmes.

The creation of new districts under a decentralised system of government ought to be approached with great caution, considering the need to make the district councils as financially viable as possible. Creation of new districts should be subject to parliamentary approval, given the lasting impact on the government budget.

Avoiding ad hoc fiscal measures

Another issue to review is the tendency to respond to problems by pre-empting financial resources through the creation of special funds, such as the proposed Education Fund. Sustained improvement in social services is best based on the long term ability to manage the government's resources through the budget. Special funds create distortions in planning of priorities in the allocation of limited government resources and create arbitrary tax burdens on those who are designated to pay. One cannot create a special fund every time there is a heightened national awareness of a problem.

Greater support for non-government service provision

The private sector and voluntary and other non-governmental organisations should be encouraged to continue to participate in the provision of social services and the building up of the economic infrastructure. The civil service and local government needs to play a more supportive role, encouraging and facilitating the non-governmental provision of services.

Judicial reform

One governance issue that can be tackled immediately with modest financial costs is the reform of the judiciary. This may involve the appointment of more staff (a 47 percent shortage in primary court magistrates has been reported).

Enforcement of anti-corruption measures

The implementation of the Warioba Report recommendations needs to be carried out with greatly increased vigour with the public fully informed of progress. The disclosure of assets by public figures needs to be followed up with verification and periodic evaluation of their status. A fresh start may be required in the enforcement of anti-corruption measures. By granting amnesty to those who admit past failing and renounce further involvement in unlawful practices (including tax evasion), a line could be drawn under the past, after which new standards should be enforced with a credible level of commitment.

Strengthening the Bunge

Efforts may be required to strengthen the capacity of parliamentarians to debate and analyse government documents and draft new laws (by providing better library facilities and supporting staff). The independence of backbench MP's is critical to the effective operation of the Bunge; it is therefore debatable whether the appointment of MPs in boards of directors of state enterprises and organisations is compatible with their role as overseers of government.

Improved management of aid to NGOs

There may be a need for a national framework agreement between NGOs and the Government on the NGOs' relationship with foreign agencies in order to safeguard the independence of NGOs. Better guidelines are required for decentralised aid mobilisation to ensure that:

(a)   projects financed reflect the genuine priority of the concerned community;
(b)   projects are sustainable after termination of donor financing;
(c)   projects are executed using local capacities and resources;
(d)   effective accountability for use of funds is established; and
(e)   projects should be replicable, so as to spread the benefits.

Such guidelines should be drawn up after appropriate consultation with donors and national bodies representing local communities and NGOs.

A code of conduct on religious freedom

In recent years the government has been dragged into religious conflicts.

This is extremely dangerous. A very clear policy of government non-involvement in religious disputes needs to be drawn up, with a code of conduct for public servants, politicians and former national leaders. The same code of conduct should clarify the supplementary role religious organisations can play in offering social services such as education and health, and the limits they have to observe in engaging in trade and other economic activities while still enjoying tax privileges. In view of escalating internal conflicts within religious organisations, which can overflow and disturb civil order, the government should initiate a process to encourage religious groups to have clear internal governance mechanisms for resolving conflicts.

In Tanzania aid has never been very effective in stimulating growth. There are three particular reasons why it may continue to be ineffective:

(a) *The decreasing growth component of aid programmes:* After a period in which donors have been supporting a much reduced role for government, there has been a tendency for donors to add to the policy agenda a range of charitable and other paternalistic objectives. Aid has become increasingly concerned with the promotion of an agenda which finds favour amongst the pro-aid lobbies in the donor countries - concerns for democracy, poverty, gender and the environment, rather than economic growth as such. While all these concerns may be of merit, they do not necessarily provide the basis for a practical programme in light of acknowledged capacity constraints.[44]

(b) *The erosion of national capabilities and ownership:* Aid dependence has contributed to the erosion of the capability of government to take effective initiatives. The 'development programme' is largely made up of donor financed and designed projects and policy initiatives originate with the donor agencies.

(c) *The distortion of incentives:* It has been argued, that in the early 1980s aid had an indirect Dutch disease effect, underwriting a distorted policy regime (allowing the authorities to postpone exchange rate adjustment). Since that time, the impact of aid on exchange rate levels has been problematic. Apart from such possible macroeconomic effects, aid has had a strong impact on the incentive system, particularly for the educated elite. Be it acquiring a grant, launching an NGO to attract donor support, acquiring jobs in donor funded project units, or simply attending courses, workshops and seminars, aid has become an important source of income for the educated elite. The concern here is that the relatively soft market for services by donors may direct energies away from the riskier, more challenging arena of entrepreneurship in the commercial economy.

Trends in aid

Since the 1970s, Tanzania has been heavily reliant on official bilateral and multilateral aid for financing its development programmes and for supporting its balance of payments. Multilateral donors include the IMF, World Bank, ADB, EU, UNDP, IFAD, WFP and UNHCR, while the major bilateral donor countries are Japan, UK, Denmark, Norway, Netherlands, USA, Sweden, China, Canada, Italy, Germany, Switzerland, Ireland and Finland. Table 16 shows aid flows for the period 1970-97 which, in total, amount to about US $17 billion.

Table 16: Aid Flows to Tanzania Between 1970-1998 (in US $ million)

Year	Total Bilateral	ODA Multilateral	Total Aid	Share of Bilateral Aid in Total Aid
1970-74	372	66	438	85%
1975-79	1493	406	1899	79%
1980-84	2339	776	3115	75%
1985-89	3080	856	3936	78%
1990-94	3307	1836	5145	64%
1995-97 (NB:3 years)	1385	1196	2581	54%

Source: Derived from OECD and UNDP data (various years)

According to OECD data, the volume of ODA accounts for over 80 percent of net total inflows of external capital, suggesting that private capital inflows have been small. The annual disbursement of ODA rose from US $51 million in 1970 to a peak of US $1,151 million in 1990. Since then the volume of aid has gradually declined to US $814 million in 1995.

Historically, three trends in donor programmes can be identified:

(a) The shift to programme aid. The shift from project aid to programme assistance in the 1980s was prompted partly by the growing balance of payment problems and the declining utilisation of capacity in the industrial and other sectors. Substantial aid has, since the 1980s, been disbursed either directly to projects or as balance of payments support through Commodity Import Support (CIS) and later through the Open General License (OGL) schemes. In the 1960s and 1970s project assistance was preferred to programme aid.

(b) A shift towards more explicit funding of recurrent budget activities. This shift was a response to the growing awareness that insufficient allocations to recurrent expenditure in the government budget had become a more binding constraint to the delivery of output and other services than allocations to the development budget.

(c) The growing concern about aid effectiveness and its relationship with the macroeconomic policy framework has enhanced donor interest in macroeconomic and sectoral policies. This partly explains a shift in attention towards economic management and development administration and other aspects of capacity building in policy analysis.

Technical assistance

The share of TA resources in total foreign assistance is estimated to have increased from about 27 percent in 1980-1985 to about 32 percent 1986-1988, declining to around 25 percent in recent years.

After almost forty years of attempting to develop manpower capacities in Tanzania through the use of technical assistance from overseas, it might be expected that TA would have reduced to negligible levels as national manpower capacity developed. However, experience has shown that many forms of technical assistance displace national capacity, rather than building it, so that overall technical assistance has served to erode, rather than to increase national capacity. In order to speed up project implementation, donors are frequently tempted to perform functions that should properly lie with the recipient countries. Many projects are managed outside the normal government system, with project management units forming a parallel administrative system, with their own incentives and recruitment arrangements, impeding the building of local core capacity and local ownership of development programmes. Even where donors have made a serious effort to make more use of local consultants, this has not dealt with the issue of developing core administrative capacity.

At present there is no coherent policy on the role and the limits on the use of TA. There has been little evaluation of the impact of TA on indigenous capacities, and when critical studies have been made, they have had little impact on donor practice. The numbers of TA personnel are not well documented. TA responsibilities are scattered among ministries, with uncoordinated procedures for determining priority needs, recruiting expatriates, extending contracts, issuing immigration visas and work permits, training of local staff, negotiating donor funding and evaluating TA performance. Donors directly manage TA funds, depriving the government of information.

The government has recognised this problem and in 1998 made an effort to design a more organised system for TA management to promote better utilisation of external resources for building lasting local institutional capabilities. However, there is only likely to be a fundamental change when there is a sustained cooperative effort between government and donors to change TA practice.

Programme aid

Under the ERP in 1986, there was a significant shift to programme aid. Donors provided foreign exchange to cushion the devaluation, stimulate agricultural exports, and increase capacity utilisation. Import support ran into difficulties in early 1980s due chiefly the failure to collect counterpart payments or account for the foreign exchange that the donors had disbursed.

The scheme was resumed in 1988 after some attempts were made to overhaul it, but overdue amounts were estimated to be Tshs 160 billion at the end of 1992. Around 1992 sharp disagreements had surfaced between the government and the donors over the management of aid programmes. There were reports of rampant corruption, reduced tax collection and increased lack of accountability in resource use. Since then donor confidence has been gradually restored. In 1996 the Nordic countries spearheaded a special dialogue to bring the two sides closer together. Nevertheless, by the end of 1997, there was still an outstanding amount of Tshs 115.6 billion and no substantial collection had been made by mid-1998 (ESRF, 1998).

Donor distrust was reflected in disbursements. In 1993/94 a total of 99.4 percent of pledges were disbursed. 1994/95 to 1995/96 experienced disbursement rates of 34.9 percent and 30.7 percent respectively, because most donors withheld their import support in the face of mismanagement and the government's poor tax collection. Thereafter, disbursement rates picked up to 58 percent and 50.4 percent in 1996/97 and 1997/98, respectively.

Table 17: Selected Aid Intensity Ratios in Tanzania 1970-1997 (in US $ and %)

Year	ODA in US $ m	ODA/ GOT Revenue	ODA/ GOT Expend.	ODA/ Invest.	ODA/ Imp.	ODA per capita* US $	ODA/ GDP
1970	51	22.9	16.4	19.37	16.1	3.8	4.0
1973	101	25.1	22.3	24.86	20.8	7.0	5.4
1976	263	48.5	36.6	42.41	35.3	16.6	9.2
1979	584	63.7	39.0	55.88	46.2	32.7	13.2
1982	671	61.6	36.7	43.91	59.5	34.5	10.7
1985	477	39.2	27.6	43.56	47.7	23.0	6.9
1988	982	193.6	163.0	147	82.4	43.5	24.2
1991	1081	158.1	136.9	88.4	73.2	43.9	23.3
1993	905	194.0	146.6	100.1	61.8	34.8	25.2
1995	814	116.6	103.4	76	52.8	29.6	14.8
1996	907	113.5	128.8	85	65.1	32.0	14.3
1997	860	145.3	130.7		64.3	9.6	14.3

Source: Calculated from BoT and Planning Commission data

Aid intensity

Tanzania's dependence on foreign aid grew from 1970, and increased further from the mid-1980s, after the GoT adopted the IMF/World Bank reforms. Aid increased at rates that could not be matched by growth in government revenues in the budget or the GDP. This level of aid dependence is too high, as it transfers responsibility for development from national authorities to donors. The government needs to adopt reduction in aid dependence as a medium term objective, and should increasingly seek to reject aid offers of dubious productivity.

Aid management

The aid cycle should begin with the government establishing priorities for development projects. This process should involve consultations between line ministries, potential executing agencies, the Planning Commission and the Treasury. Such consultations should lead to firm proposals to be included in the Country Aid Programme, with project writeups being prepared by government and presented to donors with requests for funding. The framework for such coordination will be the Medium Term Expenditure Framework (MTEF), which is revised annually in the context of the PER and PFP.

In the absence of clear foreign aid policy and weak management structures the reality is quite different. The difficulty the government has in coordinating aid derives partly from the complex nature of the donor project cycle. Projects prepared for funding usually require elaborate design and appraisal. Moreover, the complexity of studies and the time required to prepare projects varies considerably. By the time the formal annual aid negotiations between donors and the government are underway, most, if not all, projects that are to be included in the programme have already been the subject of appraisal and negotiation by the sectoral ministry and the executing agency. At that time, it is difficult for the national coordinating agencies (the Ministry of Finance and the Planning Commission) to assert national priorities, or to reject projects. Central ministries are bypassed at the early stages of project identification, when work is initiated through direct contact between donors and sectoral ministries. Ministerial units develop direct relationships with donor agencies in order to initiate projects related to their interests. Regions, districts, schools, NGOs and individuals also try to gain direct access to aid sources.

Local representatives of donors and even officials from headquarters react positively to such practices, having little faith in government coordination capacity and being eager to push activities in areas they deem appropriate. A solution to this problem has been proposed under a programme called the Aid Management and Accountability Programme (AMAP) initiated in 1997, which is intended to improve aid coordination by the government. Further efforts are under way to develop a country assistance strategy that can provide a tighter framework for aid coordination.

Yet aid projects and programmes continue to be executed in accordance with donor modalities, which vary significantly among the donors.

Aid is coordinated in three ways: (a) between the government and the donors, (b) within and among the donors, and (c) within the government system. Government/donor coordination is effected at two levels, bilateral and at the government/donor community level. coordination with the donor community goes back to as long ago as 1968, when the first donor coordination meeting was held in Paris. Within Tanzania, inter-donor aid coordination started in the early 1970s, in a more or less regular forum of semi-formal meetings with no set agenda. In November 1987, the GoT met with donors and agreed to set up a formal structure for more frequent government/donor coordination. Since then the government and donors have held regular quarterly meetings attended by representatives of 30 or more donors in Dar, chaired by the Principal Secretary of the Ministry of Finance.

Various government departments also hold separate sector-oriented meetings with the donors on a bilateral basis, while government typically holds an annual consultation with each bilateral donor regarding their programmes. Considering the large number of donors, the government's official capacity is overstretched, making it difficult for the government to prepare proper briefs and guide negotiations towards its own concerns.

There are two possible ways of affecting donor coordination. The donors may coordinate their own activities, or they may be coordinated by the GoT. Of these two possibilities, the former has a formal existence; the latter is very weak. However, in the final account donor coordination will only work if the government takes a strong lead; it is the government's responsibility to reject aid which duplicates existing efforts, is wasteful, or does not reflect national priorities.

GoT/donor community annual coordination takes place at the Paris based Consultative Group Meetings, chaired by the World Bank. For the first time, this meeting was held in Tanzania in 1997, thus allowing more Tanzanians to participate. Although in 1999 the venue reverted to Paris. Annual consultative group meetings provide a useful forum for exchanging information and surveying broad trends, allowing donors to examine broad policy areas that exercise their concern. Such meetings do not, however, provide a suitable arena for the practical coordination of aid projects or detailed programming.

In addition to the consultative group meetings, donors also convene under the Paris Club, led by the IMF to consider debt repayments. The OECD-DAC donors have monthly meetings chaired on an alternating basis by UNDP and the World Bank. There are also EC donor meetings; Nordic donor meetings; and ad hoc donor meetings concerned with specific sectors and themes. In recent years, donors have been experimenting with sector wide aid programmes as a means of donor coordination. In Tanzania there have, for example, been considerable efforts to coordinate donor activities in the road sector.

Tanzania organises its involvement through the Inter-Ministerial Technical Committee (IMTC) monthly joint evaluation committee meetings co-chaired by the Ministry of Finance and BoT. Monthly joint government/donor meetings under the auspices of the World Bank are the primary means by which the GoT tries to bring about inter-donor aid coordination. However, some bilateral donors question the lead role of the IFI's in inter-donor coordination, as it carries the risk of weakening the role of the government.

In government, units and departments responsible for central aid accounting are scattered among Finance, the Planning Commission, the BoT and in the line ministries which have set up special project/programme management units. coordination and reporting among these institutions is cumbersome and time-consuming. Often there are divergences in the information provided. There is a need to rationalise the structure of accountability, especially to strengthen the capacity of the Ministry of Finance. The budget preparation and aid programming processes need to be streamlined and integrated, the use of TA staff contained, and the information on disbursements improved.

The problems of donor coordination were analysed in a 1995 report compiled by a group prominent economists, familiar with Tanzania, headed by Professor Helleiner (Box 2).

Box 2: The Helleiner Report

During 1993-95, relations between GoT and the principal donors had deteriorated seriously over failure of the collect counterpart funds under CIS and to increase tax efforts. Suspicions of corruption were rife. And donors started to cast serious doubt over the effectiveness of their aid as indicated, for instance, in the evaluation studies carried out by The Nordic countries and The Netherlands in 1994. GoT commitment to reforms was questioned and failure to conclude a new ESAF with IMF worsened donor fears about GoT control of its agenda for reform, especially in the administrative and budgetary area. The GoT felt that donor demands were often unrealistic and too intrusive in matters that were essentially domestic. An independent group of advisers/consultants from both Tanzania and Europe was thus commissioned by Denmark to see how the climate of confidence between the two sides could be restored. The Group was headed by Prof. G. K. Helleiner. and presented its report in June 1995.

The report was a subject of a workshop of January 1997 involving the GoT and donor officials in Dar to try to reach agreement on the recommendations for improving the aid relations.

The main problems raised in the Helleiner Report can be summarised as follows:

(a) failure to match various interests of donor and GoT agencies with agreed national priorities;
(b) proliferation of projects and parallel project management systems;
(c) limited government capacity;
(d) harmonisation of procedures and information;
(e) lack of coordination among government agencies; harmonisation between donor country programmes and agreed priorities; and information on resource commitments and expenditure.
(f) a need to combine aid commitments with debt relief to determine financing requirements;
(g) a need for sector-wide master plans to facilitate inter-donor cooperation in the same sectors;
(h) a need to increase stability of the joint development efforts; and
(i) a need to enhance the credibility of government policies and programmes.

The issues raised in the Helleiner Report have continuing relevance.

Link between aid and debt relief

One area that the Helleiner Report addresses relates to the need for donors to coordinate assistance they provide in the form of new aid flows, with that offered in the form of debt relief. The report notes that currently there are two distinct fora (Consultative Groups and the Paris Club) involved, and inconsistencies in information may occur, for example, due to differences in the timing of the two meetings. The report recommends that individual donor countries should combine data on assistance given in the forms of new commitments and debt relief so as to enable accurate assessment of financial requirements. It further recommended that steps should be taken to reduce costs by consolidating Consultative Group and Paris Club meetings.

The GoT has given the problem of multilateral debt urgent attention. Under HIPC, Tanzania's qualification to benefit from resources of the HIPC Initiative was delayed to the year 2000. The GoT set up the Multilateral Debt Relief Fund (MDF) in July 1998. A broad debt strategy was drawn up that establishes guidelines for reducing the debt burden and restricting future borrowings. The bold decision by the Third Phase Government to meet external debt commitments has not been popular internally but has been appreciated by some donors. They have contributed to MDF and urged the IMF to advance the decision date for HIPC.

Ownership

Tanzania's aid intensity is so great it is incompatible with the goal of achieving self-reliance and sustainable development. With donors funding most of the development budget, there is a perception that no development activity is possible without outside assistance. Everyone vies for donor support even for the smallest projects. The national opportunity cost of aid is ignored, even when projects involve additional debt creation. Aid dependency is combined with weak capacity within the GoT to initiate policy analysis or provide independent professional advice to counterbalance policy proposals emanating from the Bretton Woods institutions.

Self-confidence in policy formulation and implementation is one of the most important aspects of ownership and has been emphasised in Vision 2025, drafted at the initiative of the current government. With the private sector assuming a more conspicuous role in the economy and donors insisting on participatory governance, the GoT has begun to regard consultations with outside bodies more favourably. Important policy recommendations are now discussed, prior to their adoption; with university academics, the chambers of commerce, NGOs, the donors and representatives of the media, and to a lesser extent, with the opposition parties. Hopefully the foundation is being laid for more effective national control of policies.

Ownership is not limited to dealing with policy issues alone. It has even more relevance to projects. Projects are more likely achieve their objectives when they are conceived and executed with the full involvement of all stakeholders. However, donor agencies still judge performance by the levels of approval and disbursement. This culture has, to some extent, been encouraged by passive recipients who often accept donor suggestions without question.

When donors lose trust in the ability of existing local personnel to execute projects they set up project implementation units, often staffed with expatriates. Local staff are often marginalised or are recruited into management units on special salary scales and other fringe benefits, distorting the government incentive system and shifting their loyalty to the donor agency.

In the last two years, following extensive discussions in 1997 of the Helleiner Report, some agreement emerged between the Tanzanian government and donors, on steps to increase Tanzanian ownership of the planning, design, implementation, monitoring and evaluation of aid programmes. The accent has been placed on Tanzania to take the lead in setting the development agenda. Professor Helleiner returned to the country in March 1999 to assess the follow-up to the 1997 agreement. He concluded that a new partnership was emerging, based on the five fundamental elements:

(a)   a solid Tanzanian policy platform in the form of a vision of the future;
(b)   continuous and intensified Tanzanian efforts towards democratisation, the upholding of human rights, freedom of the media and popular participation;
(c)   a steady course in combating corruption, and further sustenance of good governance and transparency in government;
(d)   achievement of macroeconomic stability and increased domestic resource mobilisation; and
(e)   continuing refinement of the role of government, focusing on core functions, and inviting civic society and the private sector to shoulder increased responsibilities and roles.

Since then steps have been taken to formulate the Tanzania Assistance Strategy (TAS) through a cooperative government/donor effort. The rationale of TAS is to formulate a Country Assistance Strategy (CAS) that can address poverty reduction as the overriding objective. TAS is expected to include a five year poverty reduction national framework comprising a national development agenda, a mechanism for monitoring and evaluation, best-practice development cooperation and enhanced predictability of resources.

Challenges ahead

A deliberate effort has to be made to reduce the relative weight of aid in the budget. Given that actual aid flows usually fall short of pledges, it makes planning and local resource allocation more meaningful to target lower, more realistic, levels of mobilisation of external funds. Where proposed aid is unnecessary or the project costs are inflated, even in case of grant assistance, aid should be rejected. Aid usually has costs in terms of local costs and an opportunity cost, when aid funds are charged against a shadow allocation or envelope of donor funds earmarked for Tanzania.

It is vital to ensure that funded projects are self-sustaining once the aid money is terminated. In the case of loans, it must be remembered that each additional one has immediate repercussion on the country's net credit worthiness and debt servicing capacity. The government needs to actively implement the national debt strategy and institute mechanisms to evaluate all loan proposals and restrain any tendency to increase the debt burden, to avoid relapsing into the heavy debt burden now being addressed under the

HIPC initiative.

For a reasonable period of transition from aid dependence, the GoT and donors need to agree to continue to fund recurrent expenditure and maintenance of existing assets and facilities. Measures must be taken to enhance the government's ownership of all development programmes, with priority being given to the Tanzanian Assistance Strategy. A more proactive role in managing TA is required, in order that direct donor management of TA programmes can be eliminated within a given time frame. In addition, a thorough review should be carried out on the whole practice of creating independent PIUs/PMUs for donor-funded programmes.

This book has reviewed the performance of the third phase government in the broad context of the social, economic and political conditions it inherited. The performance and policy options facing the government have been interpreted in relation to the nature of the whole system and the crisis it faced in historical perspective.

In the context of the selective focus of this review the following seven key points can be highlighted:

1. Need to focus

Given the implementation capacity of government, long lists of ambitious but unrealistic activities must give way to clear priorities which focus on limited but achievable activities. Programmes need to be founded on realistic assessments of the options on the ground adjusted and adapted to local realities.

2. Growth constraints and sources of growth

Looking at the basic constraints to economic growth, four main points have been made:

(a) Growth is necessary for the realisation of poverty eradication. However, the focus of a poverty eradication strategy must be to find means whereby the poor can raise their productivity and income levels in their existing institutional setting in the formal and informal economy. The strategy should provide greater opportunities to utilise more effectively the relatively more abundant resources, notably labour, in wealth producing activities. This process should be enhanced by improving access to productive resources, supportive infrastructure and supportive services. The first target of a national effort to tackle poverty must be poor rural households, with a focus on making a breakthrough in agricultural productivity. The diverse nature of the rural sector means that productivity increase will not be achieved by one major innovation but will require many changes appropriate to particular production systems and local conditions. One implication of these realities is that rural transformation will rely on efforts made at the regional and local levels. One key focus here must be investment in transport facilities to facilitate access and integration of isolated rural communities to the rest of the economy.

(b) A key task for economic policy must be to increase effective participation in the global economy. Focus must be on building the capacity to tap opportunities offered by a liberalising regional and international regime. Policy makers will need to give priority to enhancing the capacity to interpret developments in the regional and global economy and enhance the capacity to respond rationally to those developments.

(c)   Given the constraints on the output of traditional exports diversification into new exports is inevitable. Three main sources of foreign exchange earnings have been identified on the basis of their potential for dynamic comparative advantage. These are tourism, mining and industrial export processing:

i   two challenges have been identified in respect of tourism. Tourism development needs greater public investment in tourism infrastructure and greater national participation in terms of domestic value added.

ii   the medium term prospects for the contribution of mining in the economy are very promising. Two challenges have been identified: to ensure a reasonable retention of the output value in Tanzania and to anticipate its possible disruptive macroeconomic effects and address their management.

iii development of industrial export processing will need to be based on a productive primary sector and on the growth of competitive industries and manufactured exports.

(d)   Sustained growth will require higher rates of capital formation, enhanced efficiency of investment and increased mobilisation of domestic savings. In addition, action will be needed in human and institutional development in four areas: building the capacity of government institutions, investing in human resources, improving the institutional environment conditioning business activity and developing social capital.

3. Social sector development

The social sector delivery system requires action on four fronts:

(a)   fostering local level management by enhancing human and institutional capacities at the local level;

(b)   developing the supervisory and regulatory capacity for managing a more plural system (including the rapid expansion of non-government delivery systems);

(c)   enhancing broad access to social services; and

(d)   improving the quality of social services.

4. Monetary and financial sector developments

Monetary and Financial sector developments need to pay special attention to three key areas:

(a) promoting competition and efficiency in the financial sector with a view to narrowing the band between lending rates (currently at 21-22%) and deposit rates (currently at 4-8%);
(b) the need to deepen into medium to long term development finance; and
(c) broadening coverage to small and medium sized activities in urban and rural areas.

5. Private sector development

Considerable progress has been made towards realising a private sector-led market economy. Action is needed in four key areas:

(a) improving the legal and regulatory framework and the capacity for its administration;
(b) promoting public and private investments in supportive infrastructure;
(c) putting in place a comprehensive framework for the development of micro, small and medium size enterprises and promoting linkages between them and large scale operations in various sectors; and
(d) investment in the development of entrepreneurial and management skills for enterprises development.

6. Governance and public sector development

The government has made considerable strides in governance and public sector development. Priority should now be given to four key areas:

(a) implementing a clear vision of the new role of government in development and building the capacity for the redefined role;
(b) building the capacity required for more effective decentralisation;
(c) finding sustainable solutions to the problems of relations in the Union between the Mainland and Zanzibar; and
(d) enhancing credibility of the effort towards the anti-corruption action plan by taking more dramatic action against some of those implicated in corrupt practices in a more transparent way, with the public fully informed of progress.

7. Aid and donor relations

In Tanzania donor relations have improved substantially during the Third Phase Government. However, priority action is still required in three main areas:

(a) promoting ownership of the development agenda and implementing coordination of aid into a national framework of priorities;

(b) formulating a strategy for smooth reduction of dependence on aid with emphasis on debt relief, revenue generation, export development, domestic savings mobilisation and enhanced capacity for budget management and resource management in general; and

(c) in the transition period aid should focus on capacity building in terms of human resources, institutional development and capacity to compete (international competitiveness).

Notes

1 The non-African farming community was more diverse than in Kenya. The largest sisal producers were the Karimjees, an Asian family. The Greek community was important in tobacco and sisal, and there were many farmers of British origin - although never enough to exert the influence of the white farmers in Kenya. Germans were, of course, important in the German colonial period but were displaced at the end of the First World War, some returned in the 1920s and 1930s but were again displaced by the Second World War.

2 The structure might have been significantly different if the post-Second World War groundnut scheme had not failed. This was the major economic intervention of the period of British rule - it was intended to supply the UK market with cooking oil, relieving dependence on dollar imports. It is a pity the history of the groundnuts scheme is little studied as the British made many mistakes which have been reproduced in subsequent donor initiatives.

3 Note that one aspect of agricultural development in Tanzania in the 1970s and 1980s which has been neglected in the literature, which has emphasised decline in export production as a result of poor market incentives, has been the considerable success in food crop production for the market. This has not only included increasing supplies of traditional food staples, such as maize and bananas, but also considerable innovation, with the spread of rice, citrus, dairy, Irish potato and many other horticultural outputs. This suggests that there may now be much more of a trade-off between food products and export crops as a source of cash income than in the colonial period, which in turn is likely to either constrain the growth of export production, or mean that recovery will be partly at the cost of reductions in the supply (and an increase in the cost) of food to the East African market.

4 An exception might have been sisal, when Tanganyikan production was at its peak.

5 Over the past decade Vietnam has emerged as a leading coffee exporter. Deryck Belshaw argues that it was a mistake for East Africa to participate in the International Coffee Agreement as higher revenues could have been achieved by pursuing a strategy of increasing market share in a free market. However, it should also be recognised that if advice is being given to a number of producers then it is necessary to beware of the fallacy of composition - all suppliers cannot achieve an increase in market share, and an attempt to do so could lead to market collapse (e.g. the promotion of palm oil production).

6 In relation to marketing boards and the promotion of monopolistic single channel marketing the continuities between colonial and post-Independence policies are striking.

7 As classic example of where failure occurred is the 1970s World Bank designed and financed Geita Cotton project. This project failed largely because soil conditions were incorrectly assumed to be similar to those of other parts of the western cotton zone.

8 In this regard, it would be useful to know more about the mechanisms which have led to considerable diversification in fruit and vegetable production (e.g. the rapid expansion of citrus production, Irish potatoes and tomatoes) in last two

decades. These can be observed by following the Dar Es Salaam market, but such innovations are yet to be researched.

9   Of course, the classic works on imperialism by J. A. Hobson and V. I. Lenin were about globalisation. Immanual Wallerstein, and his associates at the Braudel Center in Binghamton, New York, have, over the past two decades, developed a body of work exploring the long history of the global economy. Walter Rodney's tract, *How Europe Underdeveloped Africa* was surely about the global economy and Africa. Giovanni Arrighi (who taught in Dar es Salaam in the late 1960s) addressed the impact of multinationals on Africa in *The Political Economy of Rhodesia* and, with John Saul, in *Socialism in Africa*. More recently Arrighi has addressed the broad historical perspective on globalisation in *The Long Twentieth Century*. Colin Leys and Michael Cowen, among others, addressed the impact of multinational business on Kenya.

10 Multilateral Trading System Impact on National Economy and External Trade Policy Adaptation of Tanzania. Interim Report prepared for JITAP/ITC/UNCTAD/WTO by K.C. Atkinson of Imani Development in collaboration with L. Mmasi, November 1999.

11 Wide fluctuations in food output are inevitable for climatic reasons. The cost of carrying large surpluses from good harvests is high, but if food is planted in quantities to avoid large surpluses in good harvests, then in poor years there will be large shortfalls.

12 In Tanzania there has been an explosive growth in artisanal mining of gold and gemstones and the almost weekly record of serious accidents suggests a need for greater controls and supervision.

13 Experience elsewhere in Africa suggests that the taxation of artisanal mining presents great difficulties (see *The Study of Taxation of Artisanal Mining in Sierra Leone* by B. Van Arkadie and S. Kamara, 1991, The World Bank)

14 In the mid-1960s the future prospects for Mauritius seemed bleak. The prospects for acquiring a comparative advantage in labour intensive industrial export, and the success of Mauritius as an industrial exporter seemed a remote prospect.

15 The decline largely resulted from disruption in intra-African trade (e.g. resulting from trade sanctions and the destructive effects of the El-Niño rains on transport). In addition, export industries processing agricultural raw materials were also affected by the El-Niño rains negative impact on agricultural production.

16 In examining their own success with the early stages of industrial exporting, Koreans often mention the role played by regular monthly meetings between President Park, leading exporters, and, top officials, to ease any constraints on export expansion.

17 In making comparisons of capital formation between the early 1990s and the current period there may be some downward bias in the data, as the coverage of private investment is probably less complete than for public sector capital formation (although even in relation to the public budget there is incomplete coverage of aid funded projects). However, the data provides clear evidence that private investment fell from the mid-1990s.

18 See Brian Van Arkadie 1990, 'The Role of Institutions in Development' in *Proceedings of the First Annual World Conference on Development Economics* (Washington:World Bank). Since then a number of new discussion areas have developed, including discussions on the role of government institutions (governance) and of informal social networks (social capital).

19 See chapters on Africa and Indochina by Brian Van Arkadie, 1995 in *The State in Economic Change* eds. Ha Jung Chang and Bob Rowthorn (Oxford:OUP).

20 Of course, there is a danger that the very strength of such networks and loyalties can be a source of difficulty, when they become a source of conflict, e.g. along ethnic or religious lines. Also, strong obligations to informal groups can be in conflict with more formal obligations (e.g. for civil servants, the obligation to family members or local communities may conflict with the more abstract obligation to the state to be fair and even-handed in the exercise of official duties). It can be argued that one real strength of Tanzania has been the combination of national policies and underlying social circumstance which since Independence has resulted in the country avoiding ethnic and religious conflicts of the type which have torn many other countries in the continent apart, at the same time as accommodating a reasonably dense network of formal and informal non-government institutions. The resilience of the society during periods of harsh economic difficulties and subsequent adjustment were indicative of the support systems that people call on.

21 See Ole Therkildsen's study *Watering White Elephants* for a detailed account of the failure of the crash programmes to extend rural water supplies in the 1970s, when the failure by donors and the government to take account of the requirements for operation and maintenance of the facilities installed resulted in the majority of pumps going out of operation with in a year or two of installation.

22 These figures, and those in the previous two paragraphs, were taken from a speech made by Prof. J. A. Kapuya, the Minister for Education and Culture, introducing to the National Assembly the estimates for expenditure on education for the financial year 1998/99.

23 Basic Education Statistics in Tanzania from the Ministry of Education and Culture, 1998.

24 See Social Sector Strategy, URT, 1994.

25 Figures in this paragraph are from URT, 1997, *Public Expenditure Review for the 1998 financial year for Water and Sanitation.*

26 Social Sector Strategy, 1997.

27 From speech by Prof. J. A. Kapuya, (op. cit.).

28 From Mukyanzi, 1999, *Review of the Three Year Third Phase Government in the Social Sectors and Human Development Issues*, draft copy.

29 See UNICEF 1997, unpublished report on Multiple Indicator Cluster Survey.

30 The practice of operating public sector banks as non-competing specialist (sectoral) banks was the old Soviet approach to public commercial banking.

31 Comparisons need to be made with some care, for although Kenya was the most developed in terms of industrial structure and overall per capita income, the African population had the lowest per capita income and its educated elite was

no more developed than the Tanzanian, until the effects of the crash educational efforts just preceding independence bore fruit (e.g. the Mboya "air lift"). See 'The Economies of East Africa' by Brian Van Arkadie and Dharam Ghai in *The Economies of Africa*, (eds). D. Lury and P. Robson (1969) for an analysis of the difference in the colonial inheritance.

32 One of contradictions of the Nyerere experiment was that the lack of a developed African middle-class meant that the implementation of radical economic policies faced little opposition, but the weakness of the African technical and managerial cadres meant that the capability to implement a bureaucratic-led development strategy was not there. In fact, the rapid expansion of the parastatal sector greatly weakened the capacity of already fragile government bodies.

33 Thus the recent violent attacks on Chinese in Indonesia brought back memories of the bloody pogrom which followed the fall of Sukarno. In Malaysia, the New Economic Policy favouring the Bumiputra was introduced in response to violent demonstrations against the Chinese.

34 An exception being *The Asians of East Africa* by Dharam and Yash Ghai.

35 See Brian Van Arkadie on the political economy of the soft African state in *The State and Economic Change*, eds. Ha Jung Chang and Bob Rowthorn (WIDER and OUP 1995).

36 In Uganda and Kenya, private provision of education is a long-standing practice, but was largely banned in Tanzania in the Nyerere period. Now considerably more children enter private high schools than public institutions, and the mushroom growth of private hospitals and dispensaries has grown to the point that two private colleges now offer medical training in Dar es Salaam.

37 Y. M. Tsikata and L. B. Madete. November 1999, *Private Sector Investment*. Paper prepared for ILO-IPRE studies.

38 Mollel speech July 1999

39 The airline is no longer a monopoly. It has always faced competition on international routes, and now has domestic competitors. Likewise, in telecommunications there are now a number of mobile phone firms operating, although there is still state monopoly of the terrestrial service.

40 The study is being carried out by ESRF on behalf of CMSA.

41 Controls continued in principle until the 1980s. The thinking behind the initial introduction of controls was that such expensive technology should be standardised to make repair and maintenance easier. Bureaucratic inertia resulted in the survival of the control mechanism long after it made any sense, although it became no more than a formal licensing formula - yet another minor bureaucratic irritation.

42 The figure probably includes between 14 000 and 25 000 ghost workers.

43 Report of the Task Force on Rationalization of Central and Local Government Taxes, URT, March 1999.

44 See the introduction and paper by Brian Van Arkadie and Harris Mule in *Aid: Dialogue or Domination*, eds. Kvell Haavnevik and Brian Van Arkadie, 1996.

Bibliography

Atkinson, K. C., And Mmasi, L. (1999) *Multilateral Trading System Impact on National Economy and external trade Policy Adaptation of Tanzania*. November Interim Report prepared for JITAP/ITC/UNCTAD/WTO.

Bank Of Tanzania, *Monthly Economic Review* (Various Issues), Dar es Salaam: BoT.

Bank Of Tanzania (1998) *Economic and Operations Report for the year ended 30th June 1998*. Dar es Salaam: BoT.

Bigsten, A. and Danielsson, A. (1999) *Is Tanzania an Emerging Economy?* Unpublished paper.

Bigsten, A., Mutalemwa, D., Tsikata, Y. and Wangwe, S. (1999) *Aid and Reform in Tanzania*. Paper submitted to World Bank (forthcoming).

Chang, H. J. and Rowthorn, B. (1995) *The State in Economic Change* Oxford: Oxford University Press.

Dia, M. (1993) *A Governance Approach to Civil Service Reform in Sub-Saharan Africa*. World Bank Technical Paper Serial Number 225. Washinghton DC: World Bank.

ESRF (1999) *Assessment of Aid Management and Accountability Programme*, June. Report submitted to UNDP at the Ministry of Finance. Dar es Salaam: ESRF.

Helleiner, G.K. (1999) *Changing Aid Relations in Tanzania*, March 23. Progress Report submitted to the Government of Tanzania, unpublished.

Ministry of Health/Donors (1998) *Health Sector Reform Review*, Dar es Salaam: MoH.

Ministry of Health/Donor (1996) *Health Sector Reform Appraisal for Tanzania* Dar es Salaam: MoH.

Mjema, G.D. (1999) *Global and Regional Issues In Tanzania During The 1995-1998 Period*, unpublished paper (Revised consultancy report submitted to ESRF: Dar es Salaam).

Mukyanuzi, F. (1999) *Review of the Three Year Third Phase Government: Performance in the Social Sectors and Human Development Issues* August, unpublished paper (Revised consultancy report submitted to ESRF: Dar es Salaam).

Mukyanuzi, F. (1999) *National development: Vision 2025 in the Context of the Health Sector.* Unpublished.

Mukyanuzi, F., Tibandebage, P., Kalugula, C. and Kibaya, S. (1999) *Education Financing and Bugetary Reform in Tanzania*. Unpublished.

Ndulhu, B. Semboja, J. and Mbelle, B. 1998 'Promoting Non-Traditional Exports in Tanzania' in G. K. Helleiner *Non-Traditional Exports and Development in Sub-Saharan Africa: Issues and Experience*, (Forthcoming).

OECD (1995) *Participatory Development and Good Governance*. Paris: OECD.

Royal Danish Ministry of Foreign Affairs (June, 1995) "Report of the Group of Independent Advisors on Development Co-operation Issues Between Tanzania and its Aid Donors", in G. K. Helleiner, The Helleiner Report.

Shitundu, J. (1999) *Social Economic Performance During the First Three Years of the Third Phase Government (1995-1998)* August. Unpublished paper (Revised consultancy report submitted to ESRF: Dar es Salaam).

Tanzania Association of Accountants (TAA) (July 15, 1999) *Seminar report on the*

Impact of Privatisation on Tanzania's Economy. Dar-es-Salaam.

The Guardian newspaper (July 29, 1999) quoting the Inspector General of Prisons, Dar es Salaam: Guardian.

Therkildsen, O. (1989) *Watering White Elephants? Experiences from Donor Funded Rural Water Supply Programmes in Tanzania* Uppsala: Scandavian Institute of African Studies.

Tsikata, Y.M and L. Madete (2000) *Private Sector Investment.* Paper prepared for the ILO Investment for Poverty Reducing Employment (IPRE) Project.

URT (1996) *Tume ya Kero ya Rushwa* (The Warioba Report). Unpublished.

URT (1998) *Basic Education Statistics in Tanzania.* Dar es Salaam: Ministry of Education and Culture.

URT (1998) Speech by Minister of Education and Culture Hon. Prof J.A. Kapuya (MP) Introducing to the National Assembly the Estimates for Expenditure for Financial Year 1998/1999.

URT Ministry of Education and Culture Budget Speeches (1996-1998).

URT (1994) *Social Sector Strategy.* Dar es Salaam: URT

URT (1996) *Health Sector Reform plan of Action (1996-1999)* Dar es Salaam: MoH.

URT (1997 and 1998) *Economic Surveys.* Dar-es-Salaam: Planning Commission.

URT (1997) *Public Expenditure Review for the 1998 Financial Year for Water and Sanitation Sectors.* Dar es Salaam: URT.

URT (1998) *Sectoral Vision and Priorities.* Dar es Salaam: MoH.

URT (March 1999) *National Debt Strategy: Part I External Debt.* Mzumbe Book Project.

URT (1999) *Progress Report on Social Summit Resolutions Implementations.* Dar es Salaam:URT.

URT (1999) *PSRC Annual Report and Accounts for the year ended 30 June,1998.* Dar es Salaam: URT.

URT (March 1999) *Report of the Task Force on Rationalisation of Central and Local Government Taxes.* Dar es Salaam: URT

UNICEF (1997) *Multiple Indicator Cluster Survey.* Unpublished.

Van Arkadie, B. (1990) *The Role of Institutions in Development:* Proceedings of the First Annual World Conference on Development Economics. Washighton: World Bank.

Van Arkadie, B. and Ghai, D.(1969) 'The Economies of East Africa' in *The Economies of Africa* (eds) D. Lury and P. Robson, London: George Allen and Unwin

Van Arkadie, B. and Kamara, S. (1991) *Study of Taxation of Artisanal Mining in Sierra Leone.* World Bank. Unpublished.

Van Arkadie, B. (1994) *Public Sector Accountability and Competence in Tanzania* An Issue Paper for DANIDA, December 15. Unpublished.

Van Arkadie, B. and Mule, H. (1996) "Aid, Dialogue or Domination", in (eds.) Kvell Haavnevik and B. Van Arkadie, Uppsala

Van Arkadie, B. (1998) *Good Governance in Economic Management and Combating Corruption.* An issues paper prepared for the first meeting of the expert on good governance and corruption. Commonwealth Secretariat.

Wangwe, S.M and Y.Tsikata (17-10 May, 1999). *Macroeconomic Developments and Employment in Tanzania*. Paper presented at the national round-table meeting on employment policy, Dar es Salaam.

World Bank (1996) *Taking Action to Reduce Poverty in Sub-Saharan Africa*. Washington: Oxford University Press.

World Bank (1998) *Poverty and Hunger: Issues and Options for Developing Countries. A Policy Study*. Washington: Oxford University Press.

World Bank (1996) *Tanzania The Challenge of Reforms, Growth, Incomes and Welfare*, May 31, Volume I, Washington: Oxford University Press.

www.ingramcontent.com/pod-product-compliance
Lightning Source LLC
Chambersburg PA
CBHW060444240326
41598CB00087B/3430